my **revisi⏻n** notes

CCEA GCSE
ENGLISH

Series Editor: **John Andrews**

Jenny Lendrum
Aidan Lennon
Pauline Wylie

HODDER
EDUCATION

ISO

The Publishers would like to thank the following for permission to reproduce copyright material:

Photo credits
page 24: © Road Transport Media Ltd 2011; **page 30:** © iFly Orlando – Indoor Skydiving; **page 34:** *top, l–r* © Monkey Business – Fotolia, © Fuse/Getty Images, © StarJumper – Fotolia, © SHOUT/Alamy; *bottom* © Julian Makey/Rex Features; **page 51** *l–r* © Anatoly Vartanov – Fotolia, © Blend Images/Getty Images, © Monkey Business – Fotolia, © Kirsty Pargeter – Fotolia; **page 57:** © Image Source/Alamy; **page 74:** *top* © Gatorade, *bottom* © Volvic; **page 76:** © Leicestershire County Council - for details about Quorn Hall see website www.leics.gov.uk/outdoorlearn; **page 77:** © Todds Leap Activity Centre; **page 87:** © MPA

Acknowledgements
page 6: CCEA's English and English Language/English Specifications, questions and mark schemes, © CCEA, reproduced by permission of the Council for the Curriculum, Examination and Assessment; **page 26:** © WWF-UK, extract from *Tackling climate change. An information pack for teachers*; extract from leaflet; **page 27:** *What is WaterAid?*, reproduced by permission of WaterAid; **page 43:** Alexis Petridis, 'Suri Cruise – 4 going on 40?' from The *Guardian* (25 February 2010), © Guardian News & Media Ltd 2011, reproduced by permission of the publisher; **page 44:** Paul Connolly, 'Think EastEnders is too depressing? I have a solution - don't watch it' from *The Daily Mail* online (10 January 2011), reproduced by permission of Solo Syndication; **page 45:** Tori Ball, 'From Belfast to Beirut' from *IN! Magazine* (March 2011), reproduced by permission of the author; **page 52:** Kenneth Branagh recreating the Iraq speech by Colonel Tim Collins, 2003 (from BBC series *Ten Days to War*) on *www.youtube.com/watch?v=UpdeNcH1H8A*, reproduced by permission of L A W Ltd; **page 89:** Pete McCarthy, extract from *McCarthy's Bar: A Journey of Discovery in Ireland* (Hodder & Stoughton, 2000), © 2000 by Pete McCarthy, reproduced by permission of the publisher.

Every effort has been made to contact all copyright holders, but the Publishers will be pleased to rectify any errors or omissions brought to their notice at the earliest opportunity.

Although every effort has been made to ensure that website addresses are correct at time of going to press, Hodder Education cannot be held responsible for the content of any website mentioned in this book. It is sometimes possible to find a relocated web page by typing in the address of the home page for a website in the URL window of your browser.

Hachette UK's policy is to use papers that are natural, renewable and recyclable products and made from wood grown in sustainable forests. The logging and manufacturing processes are expected to conform to the environmental regulations of the country of origin.

Orders: please contact Bookpoint Ltd, 130 Milton Park, Abingdon, Oxon OX14 4SB. Telephone: (44) 01235 827720. Fax: (44) 01235 400454. Lines are open 9.00–5.00, Monday to Saturday, with a 24-hour message answering service. Visit our website at www.hoddereducation.co.uk

© 2011 John Andrews, Jenny Lendrum, Aidan Lennon, Pauline Wylie

First published in 2011 by
Hodder Education,
An Hachette UK Company
338 Euston Road
London NW1 3BH
This edition first published 2011

Impression number	5	4	3	2	1	
Year	2016	2015	2014	2013	2012	2011

Cover photo © Richard Cummins/Corbis
Typeset in 12/13pt Bembo by Servis Filmsetting Ltd, Stockport, Cheshire
Printed in India

A catalogue record for this title is available from the British Library

978 1444 14581 6

Contents

Introduction
Welcome to GCSE English for CCEA Revision

The purpose of this Revision Guide is to assist you in tackling CCEA's GCSE English Language/English.

Let's begin by debunking one of those persistent myths to which students cling – 'I am no good at exams!' This is *not* true – there is no mysterious, magical element to taking exams that the 'chosen few' possess whilst everyone else is left clueless, in the dark. If in earlier exams you've been disappointed by your results then *honestly* answer the following questions – your responses are likely to help you to understand why you didn't do as well as you had hoped:

 Did you revise the appropriate material?

 Was your revision effective?

 Did you understand what types of questions you would face in the exam?

 Did you know how to score heavily?

 Did you work through practice papers?

 Did you manage your time effectively?

Your answers may give you an insight into the quality of your preparation in the past. Far too frequently revision lacks focus and realism; the student doesn't understand what he or she is expected to produce by the way of responses; and the importance of working to time limits is ignored. This is a recipe for under-achievement or, in student terms, being 'no good at exams'! Obviously this is how *not* to approach the business of doing well in exams. And doing well in exams is 'a business' that every student can manage. In the future, if you can come out of exams answering these questions positively then you will have done as well as you can – and hopefully recognise that there is no secret to doing well in exams!

It is the purpose of this Revision Guide to help you manage the business of exams through helping you to **organise** and **prepare** so that performance is maximised. This will be done by assisting you to analyse:

- the challenges presented by the different components within the award
- the particular elements that go together to produce an effective answer in each of these different scenarios
- the implications for writing particular answers that are created by different time limits
- the common mistakes that candidates make and how to avoid them
- your own performances as you work through practice papers and then assess your performances in these timed practice sessions.

The aim of this Revision Guide is two-fold. First, to de-mystify the four units that make up this exam so that you are aware of exactly what is required of you. Second, to assist you to prepare to meet these challenges in a focused and practical fashion.

Basic outlines and information

The specifications

The following outline of CCEA's English Language/English specifications will allow you to see at a glance what you've done and what remains to be completed. Being aware and organised will be a recurring theme in this revision text!

English Language	
Unit	**Time allocation and outline**
Unit 1: two sections (external examination) 20%	Section A: 45 minutes Testing: **Personal Writing** No. of questions: 1 Section B: 45 minutes Testing: **Reading Multi-Modal Texts** No. of questions: 2
Unit 2: two sections (external examination) 20%	Section A: 45 minutes Testing: **Functional Writing** No. of questions: 1 Section B: 45 minutes Testing: **Reading Non-Fiction** No. of questions: 1
Unit 3 (Controlled Assessment) 20%	**Speaking and Listening** across the following scenarios: a) An individual presentation and interaction b) A discussion c) A role play
Unit 4 (Controlled Assessment) 40%	**Studying Spoken and Written Language and Writing Creatively** Task 1 – The Study of Spoken Language Task 2 – The Study of Written Language Task 3 – Writing Creatively

English	
Unit	**Time allocation and outline**
Units 1–3 are common to both specifications – see the English Language outline above	
Unit 4 (Controlled Assessment) 40%	**Studying Literature and Writing for Purpose** Tasks 1–3 – The Study of Literature Tasks 4 & 5 – Writing for Purpose

The two styles of assessment used in these exams

External examination is the chosen form of assessment for Units 1 and 2. This formal style of assessment will be familiar to you (we will look in detail at how to prepare effectively for these units later in the text).

Units 3 and 4 will be tested by Controlled Assessment. At this point a brief summary of the main differences as they will impact on you will be adequate (again, there will be much more on this form of assessment later).

For Unit 3 Controlled Assessment you will be expected to prepare: individual presentations/topics for discussion; participate in discussions/ role play scenarios; and to participate in group problem-solving exercises.

In Unit 4 the Controlled Assessment responses, whether they are testing the study of literature or writing creatively or writing for purpose, will conclude with final one-off write-ups. You will have been given time and assistance to prepare a specified title over a period of weeks before each Controlled Assessment is formally written up. Each of these will be carried out under close teacher supervision and to time limits prescribed by CCEA.

The main differences in these assessment styles

In Controlled Assessment you will be aware of the Task from the outset, whereas in the exam the questions are unseen.

In preparing for the exams you will focus on the techniques required in order to answer on unprepared stimulus, whereas for Controlled Assessment the question is known and the content of the response and the techniques employed are part of the preparation process.

Tiers of entry

Tiering applies only to 40 per cent of the award – Units 1 and 2. The complete range of marks will be available for the other 60 per cent – Units 3 and 4, which are tested by Controlled Assessment.

Decisions as to tier of entry tend to be based upon which tier (Foundation being more accessible and straightforward than the more demanding Higher) will give you the opportunity to perform at your optimum level.

	Tier of entry	Available grades
GCSE English Language/English	Foundation	C–G
	Higher	A★–D (E may also be awarded)

Organised to succeed

GCSEs are generally considered to be stressful for those taking them so anything that removes that sense of rising panic and gives you a sense of being in control has got to be a good thing. Beginning to take responsibility for your own revision process is an important step towards becoming an independent learner and this begins with being organised and planning your work.

The first four steps to becoming organised

 Have all your notes filed, labelled and complete ready for you to use.

 Know your strengths and weaknesses so that you can build remedial revision work into your schedule where necessary.

 Keep an updated year planner to ensure that you have a clear overview of exam dates, modular tests dates and Controlled Assessment dates.

 Assess the next month's priorities so that you can fill in each weekly work scheme.

Planning

Before you can plan effectively, you need to be aware of just what time you have at your disposal. Look at the following **sample weekly planner**. Its purpose is to show you how to check out your available spare time.

	4–5pm	5–6pm	6–7pm	7–8pm	8–9pm	9–10pm
Mon	Games practice		Homework			
Tues		Homework		Revision		
Wed	Games practice		Part-time job			
Thurs	Homework		Revision			
Fri			Homework	Youth club		

	9–10am	10–11am	11–12am	12–1pm	1–2pm	2–3pm	3–4pm	4–5pm	5–6pm
Sat	Games match					Part-time job			
Sun	Revision								

Create your own weekly planner

1 Roughly draw out a blank version of the table above and fill in your various commitments (part-time work/sporting commitments/social and club commitments/chores, etc.).
2 Mark in the time you normally spend on homework.
3 What's left is the time you have at your disposal.
4 Answer this question: 'How much revision time do I want to put in?' **Be realistic!** This will vary depending on what is coming up both socially and academically. Your planner needs to be flexible so that if you need to

go out and miss a session that's fine – but make it up later! Once you've decided, add in this revision time to your planner.

5 All that remains to be done is to divide your revision time amongst your subjects. Do this by creating combinations of subjects that place one of your 'enjoyable subjects' after one that you perhaps don't enjoy so much. A two-week rota based on 30- or 45-minute sessions should take you through all of your subjects.

What are the essential characteristics of effective revision sessions?

- Each session is **focused** on that subject's **knowledge, concepts and skills**.
- It is **an active process** in which you are:
  o summarising/noting/listing in your own words
  o creating spider diagrams/doing worked examples or past questions
  o underlining/highlighting key words and phrases
  o testing yourself.
  Surprisingly, **time passes quickly**.
- Every revision session **starts with five minutes spent reviewing** the work covered during the last session on that particular subject.
- Every revision session **finishes with brief self-testing** on the material covered.
- It is undertaken in **an atmosphere that supports purposeful study** – ideally in a well-lit and quiet area, with sufficient space to spread out the required books, etc.
- As assessment points approach, your revision becomes more **targeted on the demands required by the particular form of assessment** you are about to face.

What are the characteristics of ineffective revision sessions?

- Having no clear grasp of what a subject's key knowledge, concepts and skills are.
- Randomly selecting a topic to revise within a subject, with little or no recognition as to why you have chosen to revise this.
- Passively revising. Examples of this include:
  o lying on a bed looking at an open book whilst an MP3 player fills the room (or your head) with sound
  o copying out notes but making no attempt to understand them
  o using an inappropriate revision internet site and deluding yourself that this is beneficial when it's simply comfortable and easy.
- Realising that you've no idea as to what the last page you've supposedly just read was actually about.

Effective revision for English Language and English

Some fundamental points need to be considered to ensure that your revision will be effective:

 You need to know **what is being tested** – i.e. **the focus**. In this case it is your skills and understanding in **Writing/Reading** and **Speaking and Listening**.

 You need to know **how** these are being tested – **Controlled Assessment (CA) or exams**.

In addition, it is important that you are aware of:

 Personal strengths and weaknesses in relation to Writing, Reading and Speaking and Listening. Be honest with yourself without being too negative. Everyone, in every subject, has skill areas that they find more difficult – so you need to objectively assess these in relation to English. This will allow you to focus your efforts more effectively!

 The differing demands of these two forms of assessment and how to go about dealing with each.

Essential pre-exam organisation and preparation (Units 1 and 2)

Before you even get near the examination hall you need to:

 know how the two papers are constructed and what you are required to do in each section – ask your teacher if you have forgotten or look this up on the CCEA website

 know how to spell your key words *and* when you may need to use them – working with a friend on these makes this a less boring process

 familiarise yourself with any spider diagrams, mnemonics or revision notes provided by your teacher

 give yourself every chance to succeed – **attend revision classes** provided by your school

 put what you have learned to the test – **do practice questions**

 get up to exam speed – you need to practise doing the questions in the time allocated in the actual exam

 ask for help – get in touch with your teacher if you get stuck with a practice question or just need some advice or reassurance (and *not* when it's too late, five minutes before the exam begins!)

 organise yourself the night before with what you actually need to bring into your exam – include a spare pen, highlighters and a pencil

 look after yourself – get some sleep and have a healthy breakfast on the days you have an exam

 leave your mobile phone at home. DON'T bring your mobile phone into *any* exams!

Understanding the organisation and preparation for CA (Unit 4)

Controlled Assessment is **another way of assessing your work outside of a formal exam**. Here follows an outline of how they work.

Preparation and research time

The actual task(s) will be given to you well in advance. Your teacher will outline a timescale that will allow you to prepare appropriately. (In all likelihood this will be a teacher-guided process that will be developed over a series of weeks.) All preparation will be carried out under 'limited supervision'. This means that you can complete preliminary work as a class, in groups or individually in school or at home as you get ready for your CA write-up.

Teachers are expected to give whole class feedback during the preparation process; and he/she will explain how work will be marked according to the assessment criteria. Each student will complete an individual response for each Controlled Assessment.

When will the CAs be taken?

These tasks can be completed across the two years of the course. You can be expected to complete the task at any point in the academic year, provided that you meet the deadline for submission. This is an issue that your teacher will control and about which he/she should keep you closely informed.

How will these sessions be supervised?

The writing up of your response to the task will be closely supervised by the class teacher or another supervisor (it will be similar to a school exam session). Candidates will work to a CCEA specified time allocation. In English Language/English you cannot bring notes in with you to the write-up response sessions. Teachers are not permitted to comment or give feedback on the work in this final phase. This is to ensure that the work produced and submitted is yours alone. Once this is completed the work will **not** be returned to you.

Producing and marking the final piece of work

Responsibility for planning each final piece of work lies entirely with you. Your teacher will mark the finished pieces using mark schemes supplied by the exam board. Samples of the work from each school will then be moderated by CCEA to ensure that the same standards have been applied to all students taking the CAs.

Essential organisation and preparation for CA in Unit 4

This falls into two phases: (a) the longer research and preparation stage; (b) the final time-bound writing-up session.

The research and preparation stage

During this stage of the process, it is important that you:

- research and gather ideas, ensuring that your research sources are correct

- focus your own ideas on the topic

- combine, refine and order this material

- keep referring back to the question

- develop your material into a strategy or approach that will allow you to produce a thoughtful and appropriate response

- pay particular attention to how you intend to start and finish (don't try to write out the complete thing and learn it off by heart – it isn't practical or sensible!)

- prepare a response that covers all aspects of the task – remember that your answer has to be written within a specified time limit so prioritise, rather than feeling you have to get everything down on paper!

The writing-up session

During this stage of the process, it is important that you:

- get your plan down on paper first of all – this is one of those occasions where you will have plenty to write

- use Standard English (only in exceptional situations and for particular effects will you not write in Standard English)

- use appropriate connectives that highlight the thread running through your writing

- use proper sentences (including a variety of types and length) and break your writing into paragraphs

- acknowledge all sources and quotations

- leave some time at the end for checking your work: look for spelling, punctuation and layout errors/any grammatical errors and check that you have made your meaning clear

- keep an eye on the time!

On the opposite page you will find a checklist that will assist you to progress logically through the business of developing effective responses to CA tasks.

Revision Planner ✓

1 PLANNING	understand the task	☐
	know how long you have to complete the task	☐
	know what layout and format it must take	☐
	know how the marks are to be awarded	☐
	list the main aspects of the topic and select the key words – a 'spider chart' may be helpful	☐
	make a plan with an introduction, middle and conclusion	☐
2 FINDING	discuss your ideas with other people, including your teacher	☐
	list all the things that you will need	☐
	make a list of all the sources of information that will help you in your task: books, websites, newspapers, magazines, DVDs and any other materials. Your teacher may also be a source of appropriate information	☐
3 SELECTING	select appropriate information from your sources and keep detailed notes as you go along	☐
	prioritise your material – how much can you physically include given the time limits?	☐
4 ANALYSING	having selected your material and information, decide upon the most suitable approach	☐
5 PRESENTING	put your name on every page and that each page is numbered	☐
	put the title at the top of the first page	☐
	put the ideas and material clearly and fluently into your own words	☐
	ensure that the layout and format are suited to the task throughout	☐
	check that your spelling, punctuation and grammar are correct	☐
6 SELF-EVALUATING	take note of any comments and advice from your teacher during the process consider how others approach the task and how you would undertake a similar task in the future	☐

Unit 1

Section A: Personal Writing

There will be **one** task on this section of Unit 1. You have **45 minutes** to spend on this task and a further 45 minutes to spend on Section B.

Remember to manage your time properly. This task is worth the same number of marks as Section B so make sure you stick to the time limit of 45 minutes!

The **quality** of your writing is key not the quantity. You should, however, aim to write between one and two sides for this Section A task – this would be average for someone who writes about eight words per line.

Timing tips

 Make sure you keep checking the clock in the exam hall or bring a watch with you and set it on your desk so that you can keep a close eye on your time.

 Before you begin Section A, look at the time and calculate at what time you should finish the section. For example, if your exam starts at 1:30pm you should write 2:15pm on your page. This will help to ensure that you stick to your time rigidly.

 When approaching this personal writing task, you may want to organise your time in the following way:
- 5–10 minutes planning your response to the task
- 25–30 minutes writing your response
- 5 minutes checking your work at the end.

 Make sure you move on to Section B after 45 minutes! Students often make the mistake of spending more time on Section A than on Section B. Remember, if you spend 10 minutes more on Section A, you are leaving yourself only 35 minutes to complete Section B — and that's not enough!

The Assessment Objectives

Assessment Objectives are indirectly very important to you as a student as they are what the examiner is looking for in your answer. By reading them you can understand what you are expected to do in order to score well. You can use them to guide you as you revise. In Personal Writing they are:

i) Writing clearly, effectively and imaginatively to engage the reader.

ii) Using a style that matches vocabulary to purpose and audience.

iii) Organising ideas/information logically into sentences and paragraphs.

iv) Making use of language and structural features for effect.

v) Using a range of sentence structures as well as punctuating and spelling accurately.

What will you be asked?

You will be asked to produce a single piece of writing on a given subject. You may be required to write in one of a variety of forms:

- magazine article for your school magazine
- letter to a friend or a local newspaper
- speech or presentation to other students, or
- personal essay for the examiner.

The task will make clear as to which **form** you are to use and who your **target audience** is to be.

It is vital that you focus on the task closely so that you write using the correct form and address the specified audience. Both of these things will influence the **language** that you use and the **tone** that you employ. The examiner will be assessing how successful you are in both of these areas – look at ii) in the Assessment Objectives on page 14.

When you first read the task, sort out the **form** that your writing should take and the **audience** for your piece of writing. In addition, think about the **purpose** of your writing.

Let's take a look at a typical task that can be used to highlight these issues:

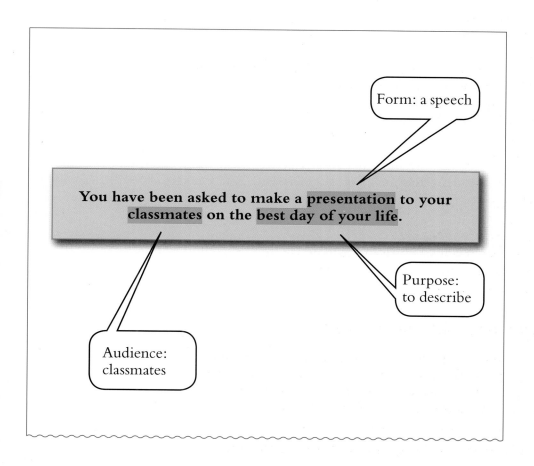

Managing your 45 minutes of writing

So, you have read the task, identified the form, audience and purpose. You are keeping a close eye on the clock and you know what time you have to finish. What are the next steps?

1 Plan before writing [5–10 minutes]

- Begin by taking this time to think about the topic and plan your answer.
- Jot down your ideas. You can use the paper itself or a page in your answer booklet. Remember that your rough work will not be marked so don't worry about writing neatly! In addition, write in note form so that you are not wasting time writing lots of words. Nobody else needs to understand your notes so be brief!
- Before you have got near the exam hall you should have worked out the way that you plan: you could use a bullet-point list, a spider diagram or a flow chart to name just a few possibilities. Plan in a way that suits you.
- Try to group ideas together logically so that your piece flows. The examiner is looking for a piece of writing that is clearly organised.
- Jot down language and structural features that you could include to make your writing engaging and interesting.
- As you are about to start, focus once more on the form, purpose and audience to remind yourself of the style and tone of writing that you should employ to meet the demands of the task.

2 Writing your answer [25–30 minutes]

Keep it real!

If you are asked to write:

- a speech, imagine that you are actually going to deliver it to the specified audience
- a letter, imagine that it will be posted immediately after the exam
- about a personal experience, use one that is real. You waste valuable time making things up! By treating the task in this way your writing will be convincing and much more likely to engage and entertain the examiner.
- a magazine/newspaper article, imagine the article will actually be published.

Remember your audience

The specified **audience** will dictate how you approach the task.

- Writing a speech/presentation: make sure you acknowledge your audience: *Friends/Classmates/Ladies and gentlemen, it gives me great pleasure to share with you one of the best days of my life. . .* In addition use techniques that will engage your audience as you address them, such as rhetorical questions, personal anecdotes and humour if appropriate. You don't want your audience to be bored!
- Writing letters and articles to a magazine or newspaper: if writing to a magazine or newspaper, remember that your audience will be the readers of the publication not the editor.
- Personal experience/situation: remember that your audience is the reader (the examiner).

Remember that the real audience of your piece is the examiner who will be assessing your ability to match your writing to the specified audience.

Writing techniques

When you are planning your work, think carefully about the writing techniques that are available to you. Remember the examiner is looking out for these techniques within your work so use a range of them to maximise the effectiveness of your piece. Of course, not all of these will be appropriate for every piece of writing. What you choose to include will depend on the form, purpose and audience specified. Below is a list of some of the writing techniques that you could use in your answer. As you prepare for your other English Units you will learn other techniques. Don't be afraid to use them in this Unit too.

- **Rhetorical questions:** rhetorical questions directly engage your audience. *Do you think it is right that many people struggle to make ends meet while investment bankers earn thousands of pounds in bonuses each year?*
- Create a **rapport** with your audience by addressing them directly: *I don't agree with it, do you?* or *Friends/Fellow classmates. . .*
- **Emotive language:** strong feelings are evoked through this technique. *The malnourished skeletal youth struggled to his feet.*
- **Indirect involvement:** *'Imagine. . .Think of. . .Picture. . .* The audience will be engaged through your use of this technique
- **Hyperbole:** exaggeration of key points can be very effective. *If my mum finds out she'll kill me.*
- **Assertive language:** *Everybody knows. . .It is undeniable that. . .*
- **Repetition:** *Homework! Homework! Homework! That's all we ever hear!* Repetition provides drama and can be used to really emphasise your point.
- **Alliteration:** *Proper preparation is the only way to avoid poor performance.* Repetition of consonant sounds makes your writing more memorable.
- **Statistics:** these add authenticity to your writing, as they are facts used to support your points. *There has been a 30 per cent increase in the number of complaints received over the past year.*
- **Humour:** very effective when used appropriately – it lightens tone and can be very engaging for an audience.
- **Personal anecdote:** *Just yesterday I was walking home from school and was appalled by the amount of litter on the footpaths.* This technique is personal so will inevitably interest your audience.
- **Tone:** think carefully about the tone that you adopt. It must suit the audience and purpose. It can be angry, shocking, disgusted, happy or reflective.
- **Effective opening:** remember that the opening of your piece will provide the examiner with the first impression of your work so it should be interesting. You may want to open with one of the techniques described in this list.
- **Strong conclusion:** conclusions are equally important as they leave a lasting impression of your work. You want to make sure that your piece engages the examiner right up to the last line!

Paragraphing and sentence structures

Your plan will have allowed you to organise your content into paragraphs. Take care to open each of these paragraphs in such a way as to draw the reader along with you. Here are a few examples: *Leading on from this is. . . Of course an entirely different viewpoint. . . Is there anyone in the world who likes turnip?*

You should aim to vary your sentences in terms of length and structure in order to improve the quality of your writing which will help to engage the examiner's interest. Consider employing the effects created by the following:

- Use of **short sentences**: short, punchy sentences provide dramatic effect. They can be particularly engaging at the beginning or end of a piece of writing or when they follow a longer sentence as they really stand out which is effective.
- Use of **longer sentences**: these allow you to provide detail and are particularly useful for descriptions.

Punctuation

Your use of punctuation is your way of communicating to the examiner how your work should be paced and can reflect how you want your work to sound, so make sure you vary it purposefully.

Think about the range of punctuation available to you, including full stops, commas, colons, semi-colons, exclamation marks and question marks.

- **Full stops and commas:** these basic forms of punctuation generally do not present problems so they will not be considered here.
- **Colons:** firstly, they are used to introduce lists. There are three things you need to bring: your passport, money and sun cream. The first clause explains that three things are needed and the second part after the colon lists the three things. Colons can also be used to provide a definition or explanation. Student: a person who studies a subject.
- **Semi-colons:** used when you want to form a bond between two statements. The statements are usually related to each other or are in contrast to one another. Typically the two statements that you link using a semi-colon could stand alone as separate sentences. For example, Nobody in the room looked; we were all scared by what we would see before us.
- **Exclamation marks:** these allow you to express emotion within your writing: It was such a surprise!
- **Question marks:** they are used to denote a question. Questions can be used very successfully to engage the audience as they allow you to speak directly to them – I don't see a happy future for them, do you?

Vocabulary

Choose your words carefully! If something is 'a joy and delight that makes the heart sing' then say so, rather than limply describing it as 'good'.

3 Checking it yourself [5 minutes]

When you have finished writing think about the following issues as you carefully re-read what you've just written and make the necessary changes:

- Make sure there are no careless errors in spelling.
- Have you included some extended vocabulary?
- Have you used a range of writing techniques such as rhetorical questions, repetition and emotive language?
- Have you included full stops, semi-colons and commas? Have you used punctuation deliberately for effect?
- Have you used different types of sentences for impact?
- Have you paragraphed your writing? If not, carefully decide where you want to make the breaks and mark them with '//NP'.

If you haven't made any changes then you've missed things!

Check your understanding – Unit 1A: Personal Writing

☐

1 I have a clear understanding of the timescales for this task ☐

2 I have developed my understanding of/competence in planning and know if I am going to use bullet points, a flow chart, a spider diagram or another strategy that works for me ☐

3 I understand how connectives can improve my writing ☐

4 I can use different types of sentences and understand the impact these will have within my writing ☐

5 I have developed my vocabulary by learning new words that I can use confidently ☐

6 I have learned to think carefully about the use of punctuation and can use it purposefully and effectively ☐

7 I have learned key/common words that I had difficulty spelling ☐

8 I have thought about the writing techniques that would be suited for the different forms of writing that I might be expected to use in this task ☐

9 I can confidently paragraph my writing based on my plan ☐

10 I prepared by experimenting with openings and conclusions ☐

11 I have practised doing these types of tasks by setting aside 45 minutes at home to complete these types of tasks under exam conditions. I have asked my teacher to look at this extra work or I've asked a friend/family member to read my work to give me some feedback on my performance ☐

Using practical sessions for improvement

Below is a list of sample questions that will help to prepare you for the examination. Aim to answer them under exam conditions – i.e. make sure you stick to the time limit of 45 minutes!

Look over your written response the next day to assess its strengths or have a friend/brother/sister/parent/teacher go over it with you.

Take confidence from what you've done well and recognise where you can improve next time!

Practical session 1

You have been asked to write an article for the school magazine on a trip that you have participated in during your time at school.

Practical session 2

A local newspaper has asked students to describe what they enjoy most about school. You have been selected to write this article.

Practical session 3

You have been asked to give a presentation to Year 11 students to help them to prepare for their GCSE examinations.

Practical session 4

You have been selected to address the teachers in your school on what engages you most in the classroom.

Practical session 5

Write an essay for the examiner about your favourite possession.

Practical session 6

Write an essay for the examiner about your memories of primary school.

Practical session 7

Write a diary entry that provides an account of an eventful day in your life.

Practical session 8

You have been asked to write a speech to present to your classmates on your future chosen career.

Unit 1

Section B: Reading Multi-Modal Texts

The focus of this examination question is to **compare** material from **two** multi-modal texts. In the examination you will have **45 minutes** to complete two tasks. Examples of multi-modal texts are:

DVD covers	Websites
Leaflets	**Magazine covers**
Advertisements	Posters
Flyers	Brochures

In this **comparison** examination question, you must:

- explore how the writers communicate their ideas and perspectives
- comment on how the writers use presentation and language
- include examples to illustrate the points you make.

In two tasks you will be asked to look closely at two main areas:

- the use of **presentational devices**
- the use made of **language** in the texts.

It is worth noting, even at this early stage, that these two tasks do not carry the same weighting. The analysis of language carries more marks and therefore will be afforded a greater share of the 45 minutes you have at your disposal. The questions that follow are similar to the ones you will be asked:

- Task: **Compare how** <u>presentational devices</u> are used to help the texts achieve their **purpose** for their **audience**.
- Task: **Compare how** <u>language</u> is being used. What **effects** are being created and for what **purpose**?

These types of questions require a **considered, reflective and insightful response supported by examples** from the text.

- You need to be able to identify the **methods** the writers have used to create the important elements within the texts.
- You will also need to be able to discuss the **effects** of these methods on the audience – and, of course, the **purpose** behind these effects.

The analysis of multi-modal texts

In most multi-modal texts, **presentation** and **layout** are always carefully chosen to aid the audience in following and understanding the text. Ask yourself *how* the text's presentation and layout help it **appeal to its audience** or **achieve its purpose**.

Multi-modal texts have a series/combination of purposes:

to entertain	to explain
to inform	to advise
to persuade	to instruct

The layout and presentation of a text is a part of its **form**. Form refers to the way a text looks and helps the content (i.e. meaning) of the text in various ways, perhaps to make the text **easier to navigate**, or **clearer for the reader**.

In order to work out **how** the text employs detail and information, ask yourself the following questions:

- How are **facts** being used? Frequently in multi-modal texts that are intended to be persuasive, they are carefully selected and presented in a way that portrays the 'product' in its best possible light – they are **biased**.
- How are **opinions** presented? In persuasive texts, opinions are *never* balanced and are given a sense of authority and influence. Work out how this is being done. It's important to be able to **sort out fact from opinion** and to be able to judge **how balanced or otherwise the facts and opinions really are**.

The range of methods used to create effects

Use of presentational devices

- **Layout** can be used to aid understanding and to make the piece more eye-catching.
- Catchy and/or eye-catching **titles** capture the reader's attention.
- **Colour** adds eye-appeal, impact and emphasis.
- Different **font styles and sizes** are important in attracting and directing the reader's eye.
- **Headlines**, captions and subheadings add impact and clarity.
- **White space** creates clarity and attractiveness.
- **Short paragraphs and sentences** are easier to follow and grasp.
- **Bulleted** or numbered lists aid clarity.
- **Formatting**: bold, italic and underline can create emphasis and impact.
- **A logo** can create a high level of trust in a product or service.
- **Illustrations** and photos add interest, clarity and emotional impact.
- **Graphs** and charts ease understanding.
- **Cartoons** add humour and attract attention.
- **Maps** may be helpful in certain cases.

Use of language

- **Rhetorical language:** increases the persuasiveness of a text.
- **Emotive language:** to create an emotional response from the reader.
- The use of the **personal pronoun** 'you' for direct address. This adds a personal touch and engages the reader; it sounds friendly, inviting and even confiding.
- **Personal viewpoint** or 'direct address' (for example 'I'm sure many of you will know how I felt that day'...) can create a friendly tone and involve the reader.
- The use of the **inclusive pronoun** 'we' can make the reader seem to be a part of a special group of people (for example, 'We're all in this together, aren't we?').
- The use of interesting, short **anecdotes** adds interest and engages the reader (for example, 'Let me tell you about the time I went to Paris ...').
- The use of **hyperbole** can create a persuasive impact (for example, 'This is an absolutely fantastic experience which will blow your mind away!').
- **Description** creates **imagery** that can be very engaging and involving, even persuasive. It can be made very vivid and used to create mood and emotion (for example, 'Like a sphere of shiny steel, the sun floated in the heavens'). Look for the use of effective **metaphors**, **similes** and **emotive language**.
- **Facts** and **opinions** are used to support a writer's point of view or argument but you must be able to separate *worthwhile* from *biased* facts and facts from *factually stated opinions*, always exploring how reasonable and effective the evidence really is.
- **Rhetorical questions** engage and help to persuade the reader. They help make a point in a more powerful and emotional way.
- **Repetition** and **lists of three** can be effective persuasive devices.
- **Tone**: a formal tone can add authority and sound authentic or sincere. An informal, or even conversational tone, can add warmth and enjoyment.
- **Quotations** and evidence from expert sources are used to provide support and create added authority.
- **Sentence style** can be varied to add interest.
- **Captions** add meaning and steer the reader to respond in a certain way to an illustration or a photograph.

Practical session for improvement

1 Look at the examples of **presentational devices** below and circle any that have been used in the *Truck & Driver* poster above.

bold/underlined/italic text	varied font style	large font	charts
diagrams	graphs	tables	subheadings
pictures	photographs	headings	paragraphs
bulleted or numbered lists	hyperlinks	logo	columns
colour	uppercase text	text boxes	white space

2 Copy out a table like the one below. Use the first column to list any aspects of the presentation in the poster which you think help it to do its job well. In column 2, briefly note how each example positively affects the reader.

Presentational device	Explanation

3 In 10–12 minutes, write a response that analyses how the writer of the advertisement has used presentational devices to persuade and attract the reader.

4 Look at the examples of **language devices** below and tick any that have been used in the *Truck & Driver* poster.

Feature of persuasive writing	Meaning	Used in poster
Imperative verbs	Verbs used at the beginning of a sentence to give a command.	
Pronouns	Use of 'you' or 'we' to involve the reader.	
Statistics	Facts that use numbers or percentages.	
Emotive language	Words and phrases meant to arouse strong feelings such as shock.	
Expert opinion	Quotations of an expert or an official organisation to support the writer's point of view.	
Repetition	Words or phrases used more than once.	
Hyperbole	Exaggerating through choosing particular words or saying something is the best or the worst.	
Assertion	Stating something as if it were a fact.	
Triples	Using patterns of three – either individual types of words or similar sentence structures.	
Slogan/catchphrase	Memorable saying or phrase to sum up the message/the brand.	
Rhetorical questions	Questions that are not meant to be answered – they are there to make you agree with the writer.	

5 Copy out a grid like the one below. Use column 1 of the grid to list any aspects of the language in the *Truck & Driver* poster which you think helps it to do its job well. In column 2, briefly note how your example might affect the reader.

Language device	Explanation

6 In 18–20 minutes, write a response that analyses how the writer of the advertisement has used language and language devices to attract/engage the reader.

Persuasive language techniques

The following text is taken from an information leaflet for schools on climate change.

Climate change is considered to be the most serious environmental challenge facing our planet. Our way of life, wildlife and environment are severely threatened. There is still time to avoid the worst impacts of climate change, but we must act now and with urgency to curb the rise in average global temperatures. It is vital that a strong, new international deal on climate change is agreed to follow on from the current targets in the treaty, which come to an end in 2012. Even if we are successful in limiting rises in global temperature, some climate change is now inevitable, so we must find ways to help people and nature adapt wherever possible.

If you analysed the use of persuasive language in this passage you might have selected some of the examples in the grid below and commented on them as follows:

Example	Device used	Impact/Effect/Explanation
most serious	superlative	It emphasises the importance of this threat, superior to all others.
severely threatened	powerful adverb	This reinforces the high degree of threat to the environment.
we must act	personal pronoun	This suggests that we all face this challenge together. It is up to all of us to do something.
now and with urgency	powerful adverbs	These verbs emphasise the need to do something quickly, to act sooner rather than later. Time is running out!
we must	repetition	It is crucial that something is done now. Action is needed to find a solution in order to solve this problem. Adds to the sense of urgency.

The following text is taken from an information leaflet for schools by WaterAid. Draw out a grid like the one in the example on page 26 and then use the same approach to analyse the use of persuasive language in this text.

> Safe water and sanitation are basic human rights. Everyone in the world should have access to them. Yet one in eight people don't have safe water to drink and over two and a half billion live without somewhere safe and clean to go to the toilet.
>
> Without these basic services 4,000 children die needlessly from diarrhoea every day and communities remain trapped in a cycle of poverty and disease.

Analysing multi-modal texts

Multi-modal texts (for example, websites/leaflets/DVD covers/magazine covers) are created for a particular purpose. Usually they will inform people about a particular issue/persuade them to donate money/buy something, etc.

They are normally eye-catching to encourage people to read them. They may contain factual information to help get a particular point across, as well as trying to persuade their readers in some way (perhaps to donate money, using emotive pictures and language to make the reader feel sad or even guilty in the hope that they will give generously).

Use the following grid to help you write a detailed analysis of a multi-modal text.

Introduction	What is it about? Why has it been written? Who is it aimed at?	Summarise in one or two sentences What's the purpose? Who's the audience?	
Presentation	Are any of the following devices used to help the text achieve its purpose: pictures, bullet points, columns, highlighted boxes, colour, maps, bold headings, different sections, different fonts, italics, cartoons, tables of statistics, speech bubbles, etc.?	Are these effective? Why?	
Language	Choose quotations to show: 1 What kind of language is used? 2 What the effect of the language is?	**Is language** Emotive? Forceful? Direct? Factual? Humorous? Descriptive?	**What's the effect** Shock? Pity? Anger? Laughter? Guilt? Sympathy?
Conclusion	Very briefly sum up by commenting on whether you think the text has been effective or successful.		

Comparison grid for media texts

Use these headings (shown in coloumn 1 of the grid below) for quickly jotting down a plan and/or ideas in the exam **before** answering the question.

Features	Text 1	Text 2
Form		
Purpose		
Audience		
Main argument/point		
How is it developed?		
Language devices		
Structural devices		
Presentational devices		
Which is more successful? Why?		

Comparing multi-modal texts

Use one of the following structures to organise your response:

1　Intro
2　Compare and contrast Text A and Text B throughout your response highlighting similarities and differences
3　Conclusion

Or

1　Intro
2　Text A – analyse in detail
3　Text B – analyse in detail but refer back to Text A regularly to compare and contrast: highlighting similarities and differences
4　Conclusion

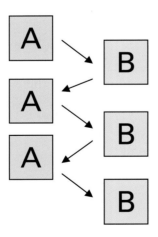

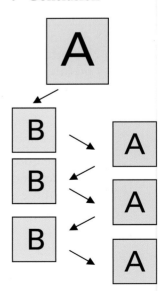

When comparing and contrasting multi-modal texts, remember to use **comparative connectives** in your writing:

- however
- in spite of this
- whereas
- on the other hand
- in other respects

- nevertheless
- differs from
- on the contrary
- rather
- elsewhere

- instead
- on the other hand
- also
- in that respect
- alternatively

Vary your language

When explaining a presentation or language device used in a multi-modal text you might say something like This image is shocking and suggests we are recklessly destroying our planet. Try using some of the following words as alternatives to the word 'suggests'.

Choose carefully from some of these to add variety to your writing:

means	creates	conveys	implies
reflects	gives rise to	demonstrates	highlights
indicates	emphasises	reinforces	strengthens

Practical sessions for improvement

The following is an example question *based only on one text* – the iFLY website page. Look at the website page below.

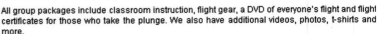

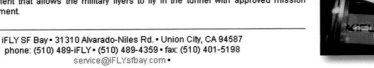

iFLY SF Bay
31310 Alverado-Niles Rd
Union City, CA 98547
(510) 489-iFLY
(4359)

Home
iFLY Explained
Flight Planning
About Us
Images
Shop

"A totally first class operation. I cant wait to fly again!"
- Monica M.

Windtunnel By SkyVenture

IBA Affiliated Wind Tunnel

© 2007 - 2010 iFly USA, LLC

Terms and Conditions
Privacy Policy

Who Can iFLY

Almost Anyone Can iFLY!

Almost anyone can fly at iFLY indoor skydiving. iFLY is safe and fun for kids ages 3 and up, no experience is necessary. iFLY is challenging for adults and exciting for teens. It is where people can experience the realistic thrill of freefall in a controlled environment. iFLY is so realistic in fact, that every world champion freefall skydiving team has trained in one of our wind tunnels since 1993.

Corporate Groups, School Groups, Parties...

iFLY is a great place for group adventure. Whether you are planning a corporate outing, a birthday party, a bachelor or bachelorette party, a school outing, or any other kind of group celebration, iFLY will ensure that every member of your group will receive individual attention to increase the fun and safety of their experience.

All group packages include classroom instruction, flight gear, a DVD of everyone's flight and flight certificates for those who take the plunge. We also have additional videos, photos, t-shirts and more.

Skydivers & Military

The advent of the vertical wind tunnel has radically changed the sport of competitive skydiving. For cost effective, realistic skydiving training, nothing can beat our wind tunnels. Flyers receive more freefall in the shorter period of time at a significant savings as compared to the cost of skydiving from a plane. The first wind tunnels we designed were built with military flyers and skydivers in mind; and that is still part of the heritage of our iFLY tunnel. We can provide a high speed environment that allows the military flyers to fly in the tunnel with approved mission essential equipment.

iFLY SF Bay • 31310 Alvarado-Niles Rd. • Union City, CA 94587
phone: (510) 489-iFLY • (510) 489-4359 • fax: (510) 401-5198
service@iFLYsfbay.com •

Task 1

> How are **presentational devices** used in this website's homepage to persuade you that iFLY indoor skydiving is an exciting and thrilling experience?
>
> Analyse the use of **images, colour** and the **layout**.

Task 2

> How has **language** been used in this website's homepage to convince you that this is an exciting and thrilling experience?

In the exam you have 45 minutes to compare and contrast two multi-modal texts. Try responding to these two tasks in 10 and 15 minutes respectively.

Check your understanding – Unit 1B: Reading Multi-Modal Texts

1 I have a clear understanding of the two tasks I will be expected to undertake ☐

2 I am aware of the timings I need to follow in order to answer both tasks effectively in the 45-minute session ☐

3 I understand how I intend to support my analysis with brief references to examples from the texts ☐

4 I understand the need to recognise the key features (purpose and audience) and how they then impact on the features that are used in multi-modal texts ☐

5 I understand and can use a comparison grid to compare and contrast specific examples of how presentational devices and language/linguistic devices are used in both multi-modal texts ☐

6 I have planned to cross-reference in an analytical fashion and to avoid simply reporting what appears in the texts ☐

7 I can recognise and explain how writers use significant linguistic and presentational effects to sustain their audience's engagement ☐

8 I understand how to vary my connectives for effect ☐

9 I know how to use quotations briefly and effectively ☐

10 I understand that close reading of multi-modal texts is central to effective analysis ☐

Unit 2

Section A: Functional Writing

What to expect

In this section you will be required to write using an **appropriate form** in response to **a given topic** for a **specified audience**.

You will also be provided with some **additional material related to the topic** which is intended to **stimulate ideas** and provide some facts and opinions which you may use to **support your own thoughts and ideas**.

Take a look at the sample task below. The key requirements have been annotated for you.

Task 1

> The **form** required will be made clear. In this case – a magazine article.

> The readership of the school magazine is the intended **audience**: i.e. mostly students, teachers and parents.

> The **purpose** is to present your viewpoint on the issue to engage and challenge the readership of the magazine.

> This statement is the **topic** or focus for the article. It is deliberately emphatic in tone so as to stimulate a variety of different views.

Write an article for your school magazine in which you present your views on the following issue:

'School children deserve healthy school meals!'

You may wish to make use of some of the facts and opinions presented on page 34 if you consider them to be relevant to your discussion.

> This is the reference to where you can find additional material which you may use to **support** some of your ideas if you wish to do so. This material, as well as the images presented, may also help **stimulate ideas**.

What to do to succeed

You will have **45 minutes** to produce a piece of writing which engages and challenges the target audience. In order to succeed the examiner will expect you to:

- adopt the form as indicated in the task **utilising the key stylistic features** of this form of writing **for maximum impact** on the reader
- inform the reader about **your views and ideas** on the topic by expressing your opinions in an **appropriately lively manner**
- **support your thoughts and arguments** – for example, with facts and personal anecdotes – to reinforce your viewpoint and substantiate your claims
- use a **range of linguistic and structural devices** to **develop a positive rapport and engage** the reader
- produce a **suitably developed** piece of writing – between one and two sides
- **organise your work** into paragraphs
- write as **accurately as possible**.

In order to do all this it is necessary to **PLAN BEFORE YOU WRITE**. Take note of the useful information and advice provided for you in the exam paper. Look at the annotated sample question below. There are **24 marks** available for the question in this section of Unit 2.

Section A: Functional Writing

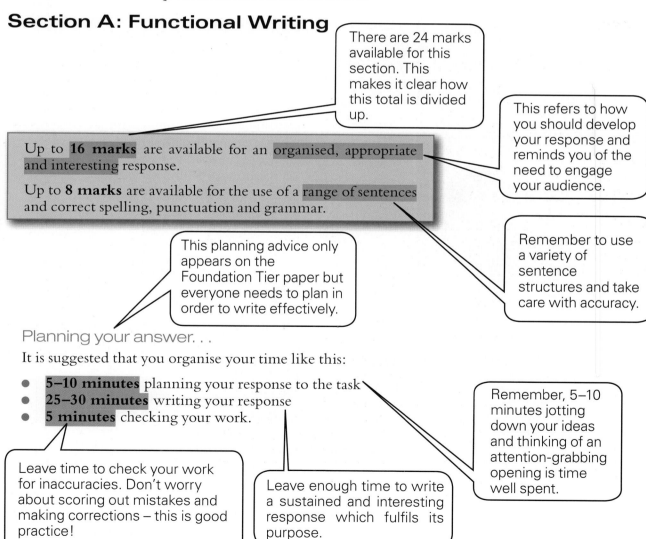

There are 24 marks available for this section. This makes it clear how this total is divided up.

This refers to how you should develop your response and reminds you of the need to engage your audience.

Up to **16 marks** are available for an organised, appropriate and interesting response.

Up to **8 marks** are available for the use of a range of sentences and correct spelling, punctuation and grammar.

Remember to use a variety of sentence structures and take care with accuracy.

This planning advice only appears on the Foundation Tier paper but everyone needs to plan in order to write effectively.

Planning your answer. . .

It is suggested that you organise your time like this:

- **5–10 minutes** planning your response to the task
- **25–30 minutes** writing your response
- **5 minutes** checking your work.

Remember, 5–10 minutes jotting down your ideas and thinking of an attention-grabbing opening is time well spent.

Leave time to check your work for inaccuracies. Don't worry about scoring out mistakes and making corrections – this is good practice!

Leave enough time to write a sustained and interesting response which fulfils its purpose.

Beside the task will be a page of supporting material, consisting of some images, facts and opinions. Below is typical of what you might expect to support the task on page 32.

"More should be done to spread the message that eating a healthy school meal is a great foundation for a kid's education and future health."

Jamie Oliver

Healthy students are better able to concentrate on their work, attend school on a regular basis and perform better in class.

Students often consume up to 50% of their daily calories at school. That's why schools have a responsibility to encourage the development of good eating habits.

A lot has been achieved over the last few years, but there's still much more to do to ensure that school food stays at the top of the political agenda.

Some more facts and opinions:

- Food served in schools meets all the latest Government Nutritional Standards.
- On average, schools spend less than 40 pence per school meal. Food for prison inmates costs twice as much.
- Salad, fresh fruit and healthy drinks are supposed to be available in every school canteen.
- Deep-fried food such as chips are now restricted to certain days.
- The number of overweight or obese 12- to 15-year-olds has risen by more than 25% over the past 10 years.
- Reconstituted meat such as chicken nuggets and Turkey Twizzlers contain 21.2% fat and are made of a pulp of skin and bones.
- Most schools devote a great deal of time and resources to developing healthier menus and promoting healthier food for their students.

How to make the best use of the stimulus information

What follows is some guidance on this in order to maximise your success in this task:

1 First of all, this material aims to assist in helping you generate ideas on the topic and to provide you with some supporting factual information. For example, the image of Jamie Oliver might remind you about his ongoing campaign for better school meals. This, combined with some of the facts provided, could be presented like this:

> So appalled was Jamie Oliver about the fatty junk being served up to schoolchildren, he decided to use his celebrity status to shame the government into doing something about it. Who could forget the look of horror on the faces of children when he revealed that their favourite Turkey Twizzlers were made of a slop of skin and bones? Parents across the nation were equally horrified to discover that they contained 21.2% fat! It's hard to believe then that crisps, chips and rubbish such as chicken nuggets are still on school menus!

It is, however, only intended to be a starting point. The examiner expects you to offer your own original points. It is very probable that you will be able to draw upon your own knowledge and personal experiences to support your discussion. This gets the reader on your side and will make your work more authentic and distinctive – and all the more interesting to read.

2 Introduce your ideas in different ways to add variety to your writing and to engage the reader:

Some people think. . .but that is not my personal experience. . .	Believe me when I say. . .
Let me tell you about the time. . .	The truth is. . .
I'll never forget the impact on me when. . .	Weighing up all these facts, surely it is clear that. . .
Consider this. . .	We need to bear in mind. . .
Imagine if. . .	I have great difficulty understanding why this fact alone would not convince you that. . .
Please think seriously about my next point. . .	

You don't need to use any of this material if you don't want to or need to. Furthermore, you will not be penalised in any way if you choose not to include any of the support material provided!

3   Whatever else you do **DON'T** simply copy out the facts and opinions you've been given – they are not a series of prompts for you to copy out and write a couple of sentences about!

Consider the difference between the two examples below:

Example 1

This reads coherently but, because it relies very heavily on the stimulus material, it would not be given a great deal of credit.

> Healthy students are better able to concentrate on their work, attend school on a regular basis and perform better in class. Jamie Oliver agrees with this as he has said 'More should be done to spread the message that eating a healthy school meal is a great foundation for a kid's education and future health.' Food served in schools meets all the latest government nutritional standards but there is still much more to do to ensure that school food stays at the top of the political agenda.

Example 2

This demonstrates how you can score heavily – by taking supporting material and developing the ideas and weaving given facts into the fabric of your response in a style appropriate to the form and purpose.

> Surely no one can disagree with the fact that if school children eat better they are going to perform better in school and achieve better grades. Clearly, parents have a duty to provide a healthy diet at home but schools have to play their part in encouraging responsible eating habits. I agree with Jamie Oliver when he said 'more should be done' about this but if the government and schools think the obesity epidemic is going to be solved by only serving chips three times a week they are truly deluded. Chips and other fatty foods need to be totally off the menu. Anything else is simply irresponsible – I would even go so far as to say that it is playing with children's lives!! We can no longer ignore the plain fact that the number of obese 12- to 15-year-olds has leapt by a staggering 25% in the past 10 years. No wonder that it has been said that this is the first generation that will die before their parents!

This shows how effective it is to combine the facts and opinions with persuasive techniques to punch your views home. Go into the exam armed with a range of these and use them to enliven your writing and to persuade the reader that you are right!

Try out this strategy in the activity below.

Practical session for improvement

Use the support material on page 34 and your own ideas on the topic of school dinners to try out the persuasive techniques listed on page 37. You could even try using more than one to really drive home your point.

Complete the following list to revise your techniques before going into the examination. The first two have been done for you.

1 **Use of a list:** Burgers, pizza, chips, sausages, fizzy drinks, crisps and the odd salad sandwich made with limp white bread – is this really the best we can offer today's schoolchildren?

2 **Repetition:** What does the average student expect to be on offer in the school canteen? The answer is chips, chips and more chips. In fact, students today think a varied diet is to have curry, gravy or cheese with their chips!! Worrying isn't it?

3 **Rule of three:**

4 **Asking questions:**

5 **Inclusive language – for example, the 'we' word:**

6 **Exaggeration/hyperbole:**

7 **Direct appeal to your reader:**

8 **Use of imperatives:**

9 **Alliteration:**

10 **Emotive language:**

11 **Emphatic statements:**

Structure for success

Effective structuring gives shape and coherence to your work. Here is a reminder of the essential structural devices you should employ.

Openings and conclusions

The effectiveness of a strong opening and conclusion in any piece of writing cannot be stressed enough. You need to connect with your audience from the beginning and a powerful ending to your response is also going to leave a lasting impression.

So, remember:

- Hook your reader with an opening sentence which he or she cannot ignore and which makes your piece stand out.
- Your conclusion is the last bit the examiner reads before deciding on your marks so go for a strong finish!

Practical session for improvement

Use one or more of the following techniques to write an effectively memorable opening and conclusion to your article on the topic of school dinners:

use humour	use a quotation
immediately make your view clear	**present some shocking statistics**
use emotive language	use a list
appeal directly to the audience	make a provocative statement
use a series of questions	try a personal anecdote

Using connectives

Connectives or linkers are words and phrases which take the reader through your thoughts and ideas. They are used at the beginning and end of paragraphs. Again, you can use these to add interest and variety to your work. Practise this skill in the following activity.

Practical session for improvement

Below are a list of connectives. Try using them in a series of paragraphs for your article about healthy school dinners:

Want to hear more?	Therefore. . .
Furthermore. . .	Next, it has to be said. . .
Let's start by saying. . .	In the first place. . .
In addition. . .	To begin with. . .
Secondly. . .	So, I believe we really need to. . .
Finally. . .	To sum up. . .
In conclusion. . .	I urge you think about this. . .

Using a variety of different types of sentences

This is another structural device to keep your reader engaged. Revise the following list before your examination:

- Short sentences for dramatic effect: I think not!
- Long sentences – for describing or narrating a personal anecdote, for example.
- One-word sentences for extra emphasis or to convey a sarcastic tone: No! / So? / Hardly!
- Rhetorical questions: Surely this can't be right?
- Emphatic sentences to convey feelings: What a lot of nonsense!
- Informal structures: Yep! Let's go for it!
- Sentences that appeal directly to the reader: I'm sure you will agree with me when I say. . . / Would you like to hear more?
- Sentences that are deliberately emotive: Fatty deposits silt up arteries and this is happening with children as young as ten. How shocking is that?
- Sentences that incorporate quotation or someone else's opinion: Who was it that once said. . . / I couldn't agree more with. . .when she said. . .

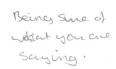

Being sure of what you are saying.

Effective punctuation

There are two main points to remember about punctuation:

1 Punctuate for effect

- It is an important means of communicating the strength of your feelings to the reader.
- It is also a way you can convey your personality and so make your writing unique.
- It creates a lively style which helps to sustain the reader's engagement.

2 Accurate punctuation

- Accuracy is an important writing skill. At the very least know your end stops: full stops, question marks and exclamation marks and use them to good effect!
- The most common inaccuracies are: to use commas instead of full stops; not to use any punctuation except for some random full stops; using an apostrophe in plural words.
- Experiment with other forms of punctuation such as semi-colons, colons, ellipsis, dashes and brackets. Some of these can be used for humorous effect.

Check your understanding – Unit 2A: Functional Writing

1 I have a clear understanding of the timescales for this task

2 I can 'unpack' a question – making sure that I am clear what the purpose of the task is, know what to do and who my audience is because different forms demand different structures and have different audiences

3 I have developed my understanding of/and competence in planning and intend to plan my work so that I know **what** I'm going to write and **how** I'm going to write it

4 I am aware of the impact of effective openings and conclusions in writing and their importance in developing a piece that is interesting to read

5 I can use a variety of strategies to interest the reader – for example, employing humour/using a direct appeal to the audience/including a personal anecdote

6 I can use different types of sentences and understand the impact these will have within my writing in effectively developing a range of ideas and arguments

7 I have learned to think carefully about punctuation and paragraphing, and how these can be used to structure my work purposefully and effectively

8 I have learned key words

9 I can employ an appropriate style and tone as well as language that is appropriate for the audience

10 I understand the writing techniques that suit the different forms of writing that I might be expected to use in this task

11 I know that I should let my personality shine through and create interest and rapport with my reader

12 I understand how connectives/links can improve my writing

13 I know to leave the last five minutes to check my work for accuracy

14 I have practised doing these types of tasks by setting aside 45 minutes at home to complete these types of tasks under exam conditions. I have asked my teacher to look at this extra work or I've asked a friend/family member to read my work to give me some feedback on my performance

Unit 2

Section B: Reading Non-Fiction

There will be **one** task in this section of the paper – it is the second task on this unit and you will have **45 minutes** in which to complete your response. Remember, just as you have learned from your revision for the Unit 1 exam paper, you must manage your time properly. This question is worth the same number of marks as Section A (**24 marks**) so make sure you stick to the time limit of 45 minutes. Spending too much time on Section A of this paper will have a negative impact on this section of the paper. Use your time wisely!

REMEMBER → PURPOSE

AUDIENCE

You should aim to break down your 45 minutes in the following way:

- 15 minutes **planning** your response to the task
- 25 minutes **writing** your response
- 5 minutes **checking** your work.

These three stages will form the basis that we will use to work towards answering this question effectively.

What will you be asked?

You will be expected to complete one task based on a **non-fiction text** that you won't have seen before. During the 45 minutes you have for this section, you will be expected to **read** and **analyse** this passage in order to write your answer. Expect to see one of the following types of non-fiction in front of you:

- Travel writing
- Blogs
- Websites
- Diary entries
- Textbooks
- Letters
- Biographical writing
- Newspaper articles

This task will ask you to focus on the ways in which the views of the writer have been presented in the text. It is vital that you focus on the question closely so that you can identify:

- *What* the piece is about – the **subject**.
- *Who* it has been written for – the **audience**.
- *Why* it has been written – the **purpose**.
- *How* it has been constructed – the **language choices** and the **linguistic**, **grammatical** and **structural features**.

Let's take a look at a typical question. . .

Read the following diary entry. The writer has expressed her frank opinions about gambling.

Analyse how the writer holds the reader's attention. In your answer discuss:

- the writer's lively and personal style
- the writer's use of humour
- the use of paragraphs and the variety in sentence structure.

Approaching the question

Once you have read the question once, read it again and this time underline the key words in the task as well as the bullet points. This will ensure that you begin analysing the key issues within the question and so help you to identify the **form**, **audience** and **purpose** of the piece.

> The form of writing (a diary entry) and the nature of the writing.

> What the piece is about – the subject.

> This tells you the writer's purpose (*why*) in this piece of writing and identifies the reader as the audience. It also asks you to identify how the writer has achieved the purpose.

Read the following diary entry. The writer has expressed her frank opinions about gambling.

Analyse how the writer holds the reader's attention.

In your answer discuss:

- the writer's lively and personal style
- the writer's use of humour
- the use of paragraphs and the variety in sentence structure.

> The bullet points give you the key as to *how* the piece is constructed – they tell you what you should be writing about. Make sure you use them to structure your response.

Your task is to take each bullet point in turn and find evidence to explain (by analysing that evidence) how the writer 'holds the reader's attention'.

The bullet points will vary, depending on the characteristics of different texts. In preparation for the exam, think about the following areas:

- lively nature of the writing
- personal nature of the writing
- humour used within the writing
- words and phrases used
- use of paragraphs
- variety in sentence structure
- use of fact and opinion.

1 Planning your response

Making effective use of your planning time

You have about 15 minutes to plan your answer. Use it to:

 read the question carefully before beginning to read the non-fiction piece

 use different coloured highlighters to identify evidence linked to each bullet point within the piece

 identify the skills that the writer has used to achieve the intended purpose as you are reading and highlighting. Don't be afraid to write these on your exam paper as you are reading to help you to prepare/write your response.

Analysing non-fiction – what are you looking for?

As you are studying the non-fiction piece you should be identifying the writing techniques that have been used. By identifying the techniques, you are demonstrating to the examiner that you know **how** the writer has achieved the purpose.

This section outlines many techniques that you should look out for. However, remember that you have also learned about writing techniques in other sections of this Revision Guide so don't be afraid to use them too!

This list is not exhaustive. **Learn** these techniques so that you know what you are looking out for in the exam! Not only will you feel more confident going into the exam but also you will be able to spot the techniques quickly in the exam.

Writing techniques

- **Exaggeration/hyperbole** to emphasise viewpoint. Exaggeration of key points can be very effective: I'm dead if I get caught.
- **Exclamations** to communicate emotion: The view was unbelievable!
- **Humour** to make the writing more lively and appealing.
- **Sarcasm** to mock the subject under discussion.
- **Rhetorical questions** to make the reader think: Can we continue to support this cause?
- **Repetition** to emphasise a point: Dull! Dull! Dull! – That sums him up.
- **Connectives** to help the writing to flow by connecting the sentences and paragraphs.
- **Variety of sentences used – simple, compound and complex** to engage the reader's interest. Remember **short sentences** are punchy, therefore providing dramatic effect. They can be particularly engaging at the beginning or end of a piece of writing or when they follow a longer sentence as they really stand out. **Longer sentences** provide detail and are particularly useful for descriptions.
- **Use of punctuation** to control how you read the piece. Remember the impact of full stops, commas, colons and semi-colons.
- **Variety in paragraphing** to add interest for the reader.
- **Descriptive terms** to paint a positive or negative picture of something.
- **Superlatives** to suggest that something is the best: The greatest.
- **Shock tactics** to frighten the reader: It's an accident waiting to happen.
- **Assertive language** to exude confidence: Everybody knows/Without question/It is undeniable that. . .

- **Imagery: similes** and **metaphors** to create vivid images which help the reader to visualise and understand the writer's point of view.
- **Alliteration** to make certain words stand out and to make the writing memorable: *The phenomenal footballer forayed into the opposition's box.*
- **Onomatopoeia** to evoke sounds through the use of words: *crash/ sludge/crunch.*
- **Emotive language** to evoke strong feelings on a subject: *The strain and stress of weeks of turmoil was etched on his hollow, pallid face as the breaking daylight illuminated the teardrop trickling down his cheek.*
- **Puns** and **jokes** to provide humour.
- **Statistics or facts** used to reinforce opinion and add authenticity to the writing: *There has been a 50 per cent increase in the number of chocolate bars sold over the past year.*
- **Expert opinion** to support what the writer is saying which makes it more convincing: *Doctor Jones stated that studies have shown that...*
- **Reference to satisfied customers** to support the writer's viewpoint: *I don't know how I survived before I bought this. It has transformed my life!*
- **Irony** to provide humour: verbal, situational, and dramatic irony.
- **Use of 'I'** to communicate the writer's point of view directly.
- **Personal anecdote** to interest the audience through recounting a personal experience: *Last year when I was on holiday with my family...*
- **Conversational tone** to add a personal quality to the writing and to create a positive rapport between the writer and reader.
- **Inclusive pronoun** ('we') to persuade the reader to agree with the writer.
- **Personal pronoun** to make the reader feel that the writer is talking directly to them therefore it is highly personal and effective.

Practical session for improvement

Let's see how well you find and analyse the writing techniques we've just read about.

a) Identify the writing techniques employed in the blogs below.

b) What has each writer achieved through using them?

Suri Cruise – 4 going on 40?
Now Suri Cruise has been spotted reading Vanity Fair and sipping a Starbucks drink. Whatever next?

Anyone who fears for the children of celebrities may be disheartened to see this week's pictures of Suri Cruise, aged four, spotted in Vancouver sipping a Starbucks drink and leafing through a copy of Vanity Fair. "She held her frothy drink in both hands as she made her way from the counter... she ensured to blow her drink to cool it down before taking a sip," wrote the Daily Mail, the level of detail in its report clearly invaluable to any reader who has never seen someone buying a cup of coffee. Lost in Showbiz doesn't wish to suggest that Suri is growing up too fast but nevertheless: Starbucks? Vanity Fair? What's she going to do next? Weigh up the benefits of a self-invested personal pension? Start complaining about her bad knees?

Alexis Petridis, *The Guardian*

Think EastEnders is too depressing? I have a solution – don't watch it.

Yes, EastEnders is the most depressing programme on television. Not just for the storylines but for the shoddy acting (Shane Richie's Alfie Moon is about as subtle as a brick through the window). If I didn't write about television I would not choose to watch it. And here's the rub.

If EastEnders, or any other show for that matter, bothers you there's a really simple solution. Don't watch it - turn over to another channel. Or pick up a book. Nobody's forcing you to watch it.

As for the pond-life who've abused actress Samantha Womack for playing the part of a mother who steals another woman's baby, well, what can you say? I'm surprised these morons can speak and breathe at the same time.

Paul Connolly, *The Daily Mail*

2 Writing your response

You should be aiming to interpret the text, showing an understanding of how the writer has used language in order to achieve desired effects by selecting examples from the writing that support your analysis.

Your response will be marked out of 24. The examiner will mark your work in relation to how well you have:

 analysed the features highlighted in the bullet points

 supported the **points** you make with relevant **evidence** and reinforced these with appropriate **explanations**.

Point, Evidence, Explain

To respond effectively you must identify the techniques that the writer has used as well as providing evidence and an explanation. Only by presenting all three elements of **PEE** can you maximise your score. Let's take a look at a part of a sample response that is an example of how you should answer this question:

> Humour [TECHNIQUE] is used to create a light-hearted mood [EXPLANATION]. The writer's use of rhetorical question [TECHNIQUE] 'well, what can you say?'[EVIDENCE] engages the reader and a positive rapport is established between the writer and the reader. [POINT, EXPLANATION]

3 Checking your response

When you have finished writing, you *must* check your response.

Did you:

 recognise and understand the form, purpose and audience?

answer the question directly by making use of the bullet points?

identify the writing techniques used by the writer?

 use **PEE** when writing your response?

 write a detailed response to the question?

Practical session for improvement

Spend 45 minutes answering this question.

Read the piece of travel writing below and answer this question.

Analyse how the writer has succeeded in encouraging the reader to visit Beirut?

In your answer discuss:

- the writer's lively and personal style
- the use made of fact and opinion
- the use of sentence structure and paragraphing.

From Belfast to Beirut

Beirut was traditionally known as Paris of the Middle East; however, in my day it was mostly known as one of the most bombed cities in the world alongside Belfast. It was with much intrigue and excitement that I visited Beirut for a long weekend. With my love of shopping and nightlife, lying on the beach and a bit of culture thrown in, Beirut did not disappoint.

I flew from George Best Belfast City Airport to London Heathrow. The flight is only five hours from London, and with a quick 20 minute transfer to the centre of Beirut, everything is on your doorstep - literally; you can ski in the morning in the mountains and lie by the pool on the hotel rooftop sipping cocktails in the afternoon. Located on the border of the Mediterranean Sea, Lebanon with its hospitality, fabulous weather and no language barrier, is an ideal long-weekend escape.

Although the war ended more than a decade ago, there is a perception that Beirut is dangerous for tourists and business visitors. In reality Beirut is among the safest cities in the world; there is almost no crime, and possibly one of the most dangerous things you can do is try to cross the road. There are very few traffic lights or road regulations; you have to just walk in to the middle of the road with your hand in the air and hope for the best. Even when you do wait for the 'green man' at the lights, cars will ignore you and drive through anyway – make sure your travel insurance is up-to-date and say your prayers!

Beirut is shopping heaven! For you travellers whose motto is 'live to shop', Lebanon is the destination for you. The Lebanese have an eye for style or design, and in Beirut, you can find all the famous cutting-edge designers in both clothing and furniture from all over the world. The Beirut Souks will cater for every taste and budget, from Gucci and Louis Vuitton to Aldo and Zara.

Nightlife in Beirut is non-stop and doesn't usually start until after midnight! Gemmayze Street never sleeps! It is known for trendy bars and pubs and is the perfect place to have a drink and watch the world go by. Head to Bar ThreeSixty, which overlooks historic Martyrs' Square on top of Le Gray Hotel – it has been voted one of the world's most beautiful bars.

The Lebanese people are warm, welcoming, intelligent and generous. From the daytime sunshine and relaxing ambiance to the clubbing and casinos of Beirut at night, there is absolutely no reason not to schedule a visit to this very special destination.

Tori Ball, *IN!* **magazine**

Below is a checklist of some of the points that you could have included. *After* you've completed your response, check to see how you have got on.

The writer's use of lively and personal style

- The use of 'I' engages the reader immediately as the writer is <u>recounting</u> her own personal experience: 'I visited Beirut'/'I flew'.
- Use of the personal pronoun 'you' creates a personal relationship between the writer and the reader. The writer uses 'you' to encourage the reader to visit Beirut, 'you can ski', 'Lebanon is the destination for you'.
- Particular words and phrases have been chosen by the writer to make the piece lively which in turn is designed to sustain the reader's interest, 'intrigue and excitement'.
- Humour is used to engage the reader: 'Make sure your travel insurance is up-to-date and say your prayers!' Even though this is commenting on one negative thing about Beirut, the use of the joke makes this negative aspect seem fun.
- The use of exclamation marks also communicates excitement about travelling to Beirut, which encourages the reader to visit, 'Beirut is shopping heaven!' and 'Nightlife in Beirut is non-stop and doesn't usually start until after midnight!'

The use made of fact and opinion

- The writer uses facts about the journey to Beirut to make it seem like a straightforward, easy journey, which will encourage the reader to visit it: 'only five hours from London, and with a quick 20 minute transfer'.
- The location of Beirut is made appealing: 'Located on the border of the Mediterranean Sea'.
- Opinions of the writer attempt to persuade the reader to visit Beirut: 'it is an ideal long-weekend escape'/'there is absolutely no reason not to schedule a visit to this very special destination'.
- Facts about Beirut's past are used to contrast it with Beirut today: 'Beirut was traditionally known as. . .most bombed cities in the world.'
- Actual bars and restaurants are used as recommendations to further encourage the reader to visit, 'Bar ThreeSixty', 'Le Gray Hotel', 'Martyrs' Square'.

The use of sentence structure and paragraphing

- Shorter sentences are used for punchy statements to urge the reader to visit: 'Beirut is shopping heaven!' 'Gemmayze Street never sleeps!'
- Longer sentences are used to provide descriptions of Beirut today: 'The Lebanese have an eye for style. . .world.' Longer sentences also explain the history of Beirut and provide a contrast between the past and present, 'Beirut was traditionally known as Paris. . .Belfast.'
- Paragraphs are used to organise the writing into topics. Each paragraph focuses on another aspect of Beirut, which guides the reader through the piece in order to entice them.
- Use of exclamation marks is effective in creating a liveliness that will encourage the reader to visit.
- Commas are used to list all of the reasons why someone should visit

Beirut: 'Lebanon with its hospitality, fabulous weather and no language barrier'.

- Semi-colons are used to connect sentences which naturally link together to help engage the reader.

Check your understanding – Unit 2B: Reading Non-Fiction

1 I have a detailed understanding of the style of answer (PEE) required to complete this question ☐

2 I have decided how I am going to plan my response when I am in the exam and I understand the importance of using the bullet points for guidance ☐

3 I have read non-fiction pieces such as newspaper articles, online blogs and magazine articles, etc., and have prepared by trying to analyse the techniques various writers have used ☐

4 I know about and understand the different techniques used in non-fiction writing ☐

5 I have practised by using the examples in this book for mock sessions, setting aside 45 minutes at home to complete the question under exam conditions ☐

6 I have used the mark schemes provided in this book to try to assess the strengths and weaknesses of my own work ☐

7 I have asked my teacher/ a friend/ family member to look at my mock answers to see how convincing my response is ☐

8 I understand the nature of the different forms of writing – newspaper articles, online blogs, travel writing and magazine articles, etc. – and the potential impact and expectations that result from these ☐

9 I know how to make use of quotations effectively and efficiently ☐

These are a number of sample examination questions at the end of this Revision Guide (pages 86–89) for you to use for practice.

Unit 3

Speaking and Listening

Speaking and Listening can be assessed across the entire span of your GCSE course.

Some of these assessments will be unplanned, where your teacher seizes upon an advantageous opportunity to credit oral contributions. Obviously you cannot prepare for these but you should be aware that this is an option that your teacher can employ.

The majority of the assessments for Unit 3 will be much more formal 'set-piece' occasions that you will be able to prepare in advance to a greater or lesser degree – and it is these that we will focus upon. You will have to deliver/be involved in:

1 individual presentation and interaction   2 group discussion   3 role play.

Key pointers in preparing an individual presentation

It is fair to suggest that nobody enjoys being in this situation. Anyone who puts on a polished presentation only does so by managing his/her behaviour. Because you are in control, how you score in an individual presentation is really down to the degree of effort you make. Here is a checklist of the strategies and techniques that you need to employ in order to make a competent presentation:

 Know what you are going to say and what order it comes in (this can only be achieved if the topic has been researched and considered before you begin to think about your approach).

 Ultimately you should have headings supported by key words or phrases that work as prompts to take you through the presentation – earlier versions might well be more detailed. These pointers are probably best put on a series of postcards as they are easier to handle.

 Take a relaxed and comfortable stance (experiment at home to find out what feels comfortable and looks okay).

 Pick a spot at the back of the room, just above the heads of your audience, where you will focus when you look up from your notes (this way your audience will feel you are engaging them in your presentation).

 The bigger the room and the audience, the slower and louder your delivery has to be! (This gives the illusion of confidence and will allow your audience to engage with what you are saying – practising hearing your own voice is a really good way of preparing your final presentation.)

 Remember PowerPoint® basics – not too much on each slide, and any text has to be accurate and easily read from anywhere in the room. Don't read out the contents of the slide word-for-word.

If using PowerPoint slides, make sure that you can change them smoothly – this process should not be a distraction to your audience – they should be listening to you and watching your slides.

 Remember, if using PowerPoint, your audience is out in front of you – they can look at your slides as you look at them (or that point you've picked at the back of the room).

 Begin by making it clear that you recognise your audience and a strong finish might for example invite questions – this offers a neat and yet positive way of concluding.

Key pointers in preparing for a group discussion

The dynamic for a group discussion is completely different from a formal presentation. In this situation remember that it is the group interaction that is central. You need to respond to a fluid situation which is likely to be unpredictable (there is no reason why it should not also be enjoyable!).

In order to make a competent contribution in a group discussion you need to:

 have researched and thought about the issue under discussion so that you have ideas and opinions to offer (it's the quality, style and thoughtfulness of your contributions that leads to high scores)

 listen intently and ensure that you are actively involved, without denying others the opportunity to be involved – don't talk over the contribution of others and invite others to share their views

 pick up on points made by others and take the discussion forward (for example, 'I agree with that, Deidre, so how can we put this right?')

 challenge points made by others in a non-threatening fashion ('I see what you mean, but how does that fit in with our right to personal privacy?')

 when you think there is a natural break or pause, try to move the discussion on ('Can I ask what the rest of the group think about the influence the internet is having?')

 occasionally, try to draw together the group's feelings on the issue ('So would I be right in believing that most of us feel. . .').

Key pointers in preparing for a role play

Like nearly every other aspect of the course, last-minute fixes will not lead to your best performance. Successful role plays are based on convincing interaction with other 'characters' within that role play.

In order to make an effective contribution in a role play you need to:

 remember that preparation and planning are central to success

 get in character – what is the situation that 'you' are in and how would 'you' react in that particular situation?

 how would you interact with the other individuals in the scenario – given the situation would you be dominant/powerful/aggressive/persuasive/manipulative/aggrieved/demanding/reasonable/short-tempered/defensive?

 consider the scenario you've been given and prepare for the different possible ways in which the situation might unfold so that you can respond – always in character

respond to the unfolding situation in character – convince your audience that you are the individual you are portraying.

Practical sessions for improvement

To complete this section, here are some sample tasks which provide the opportunity to research, prepare and check your understanding of what is required for all of the Speaking and Listening assessments – even if it is only possible to actually complete the individual presentation.

In each case, base your work on the 'key pointers' on pages 48–49. The one feature they all have in common is the fundamental need for thorough preparation!

Individual presentation

What three things would you change in our world and why?

What do you consider to be the most important piece of modern technology and why?

We all love our gadgets – but it's people that really count!

Give an illustrated talk on the landmarks that you think best represent where you live!

Group discussion

Discuss the following statements:

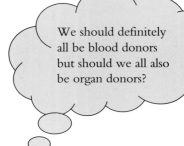

We should definitely all be blood donors but should we all also be organ donors?

We are going to be paying for the greed of bankers and developers for the next 20 years – it's not fair!

Of course students should have to pay to go to university – they're the ones who will benefit from it; why should everyone have to subsidise them?

Role play

An irate parent has arranged an interview with the school's principal for the afternoon following an incident in which she believes her son has been bullied on the bus. Following an investigation by the principal it seems clear that the 'bullying' was not as one-sided as the parent believes.

Role play the interview between the parent, principal and son.

Unit 4

The Study of Spoken Language English Language only

In this section you will investigate the way oral communication works. You will learn about how spoken language is affected by things such as place, family, class, social groups and technology.

Spoken language is one of our most important forms of communication. Every day we constantly experience communication in many different ways.

When you are preparing for this Controlled Assessment (CA) Task it is important to remember exactly what is being tested – the **Assessment Objective (AO2)**:

● Understand variations in spoken language, explaining why language changes in relation to contexts.
● Evaluate the impact of spoken language choices in their (students') own and others' use.

In this CA Task the following **learning outcomes** are what you should be demonstrating that you are able to do:

 to understand the characteristics of spoken language

 to understand influences on spoken language choices

 to explore the impact of spoken language choices in your own and others' use

 to understand how language varies in different contexts.

You will be required to study a minimum of two speeches/talks. This will allow you to make comparisons between the spoken language texts and meet all the Assessment Objectives. Your teacher will guide you on this. You will have worked your way through these pieces of spoken language in class and you will know the question you are expected to answer well in advance of sitting the CA Task.

Before we get down to looking at the taking of the CA Task, here are helpful practical pointers to remind you about the key issues that you should be addressing in your study of spoken language.

The *words* and *how* they are said

When you are studying spoken language you are expected to analyse the *words*. However, you must also remember to analyse *how* the words are said.

The non-written features of speech may reflect various features of the speaker or the speech:

- the emotional state of the speaker
- whether an utterance is a statement, a question or a command
- whether the speaker is being ironic or sarcastic
- emphasis and contrast
- other elements of language: loudness, tone, pauses, speed of delivery, etc.

The words used	How these words are said
Direct address	Intonation
Emotive language	Pauses
Hyperbole	Loudness
Rhetorical questions	Accent
Repetition	Fillers
Groups of three	Emotionally
Humour	Formal or informal
Anecdote	Calmly

Practical session for improvement

Listen to this speech by following this link: **www.youtube.com/watch?v=UpdeNcH1H8A** or study this extract from it:

We go to liberate not to conquer. We will not fly our flags in their country. We are entering Iraq to free a people and the only flag which will be flown in that ancient land is their own. Show respect for them.

There are some who are alive at this moment who will not be alive shortly. Those who do not wish to go on that journey, we will not send. As for the others I expect you to rock their world. Wipe them out if that is what they choose. But if you are ferocious in battle remember to be magnanimous in victory.

Iraq is steeped in history. It is the site of the Garden of Eden, of the Great Flood and the birthplace of Abraham. Tread lightly there. You will see things that no man could pay to see and you will have to go a long way to find a more decent, generous and upright people than the Iraqis. You will be embarrassed by their hospitality even though they have nothing. Don't treat them as refugees for they are in their own country. Their children will be poor, in years to come they will know that the light of liberation in their lives was brought by you.

> If there are casualties of war then remember that when they woke up and got dressed in the morning they did not plan to die this day. Allow them dignity in death. Bury them properly and mark their graves.
>
> It is my foremost intention to bring every single one of you out alive but there may be people among us who will not see the end of this campaign. We will put them in their sleeping bags and send them back. There will be no time for sorrow.

Using the grid on page 52, see how many examples of the strategies and techniques are employed in this speech.

Comparison grid for the Spoken Language CA

The following grid can be used to help you compare and contrast two examples of spoken language. It can be also used to make a plan for the CA Task before you undertake your one-off writing session.

Features	Example 1	Example 2
Context		
Purpose		
Audience		
Main argument/point		
How is it developed?		
Language features – words and phrases used		
Non-written features		
Personal context		
Which is more effective/appealing to you? Why?		

Preparing for the Spoken Language CA

Your personal preparation will be the most significant factor in your performance. Here are the things you need to do as you prepare:

 In your own time consider the speeches/talks in detail – what is your personal reaction to them?

 Prioritise their most significant features, as well as noting the similarities and contrasts.

 Decide how to use these thoughts and conclusions in the way that will effectively meet the requirements of the question; in other words sort out what you actually intend to include in your 90-minute answer by sorting out a realistic plan/outline on a single page (there is more assistance with this on page 54).

 Give some detailed thought to your introduction and your conclusion.

Using your time in the Spoken Language CA

You have 1½ hours to complete this CA Task. (You will be allowed to use unannotated/clean copies of the talks/speeches during this time.)

You should use the time as follows:

- **15 minutes** listening to/looking over the speeches – jotting down your plan
- **65–70 minutes** writing your response
- **5–10 minutes** on re-reading/correcting/revising what you've written.

Comparing and contrasting texts

When you are comparing and contrasting spoken language texts use one of the following three structures for your writing.

1 Basic structure

1 Introduction
2 Text A – analyse in detail
3 Text B – analyse in detail
4 Compare and contrast both texts, highlighting the similarities and differences
5 Conclusion

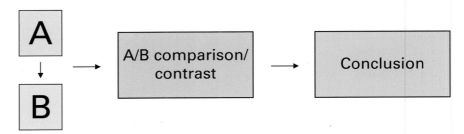

2 More sophisticated structure

1 Introduction
2 Compare and contrast Text A and Text B throughout your response highlighting similarities and differences
3 Conclusion

3 Final complex structure

1 Introduction
2 Text A – analyse in detail
3 Text B – analyse in detail but refer back to Text A regularly to compare and contrast, highlighting similarities and differences
4 Conclusion

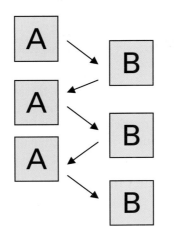

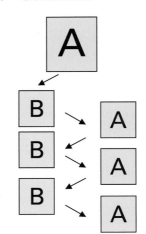

Students' work in relation to grades

Typically, the responses of students working **below grade C**:

- find an interesting feature in their study which will be described but not developed
- present points that may not to linked to the speaker's intention
- rely on quotations to explain themselves
- fail to link points of comparison or contrast to the other speech/talk.

Working **at grade C**, candidates' answers will:

- show that they understand how spoken language works
- demonstrate an organised approach, recognising some of the comparable features
- sometimes comment on language choices and how these match the speaker's intention.

Working **at grades A/A★** responses will:

- offer a critically perceptive, comparative response to the language devices used to appeal to listeners
- fluently develop their own confidently organised interpretations.

Check your understanding – Unit 4: The Study of Spoken Language ☐

1 I have a detailed understanding of the two speeches/talks ☐

2 I have developed my plan in order to answer effectively in this 90-minute Spoken Language CA ☐

3 I understand how I intend to cross reference points from both speeches ☐

4 I can use the key words such as 'purpose', 'language features', etc., so that my answer will be focused and analytical in approach ☐

5 I understand and can use key terms such as 'emotive language' or 'pause' ☐

6 I have planned to compare and contrast specific examples of how language is used in the speeches/talks ☐

7 I can identify tonal shifts and how these are designed to impact upon the audience ☐

8 I can explain how speakers use linguistic and presentational devices to sustain their audience's engagement ☐

9 I understand the significance of context ☐

10 I know how to use quotations effectively and efficiently ☐

Unit 4

English Language: Task 2
English: Tasks 1–3

This element of Unit 4 is a shared area for English Language and English. In both cases it is tested through **Controlled Assessment** (CA).

The CA Task(s) will be based on texts chosen by the English department and your teacher. The theme(s) on which they focus are specified annually by CCEA. You will study the text(s) in class and at home.

English Language: Study of Written Language (Literature) (15%)

If you are studying **English Language** you will complete **one** CA Task which will be worth **15 per cent** of your final GCSE grade. You will have **1 hour 30 minutes** under Controlled Assessment conditions in which to write an essay. The question you respond to will have been developed within your school or college. It will be based on one of three themes prescribed by CCEA.

English: The Study of Literature (20%)

If you are studying English you will be expected to complete **three** CA Tasks. They are worth **20 per cent** of your final GCSE grade. You will have **1 hour** under Controlled Assessment conditions to write each of your responses on drama, prose and poetry texts. Again the actual Tasks will be developed within your school or college based on themes prescribed by CCEA.

The style of Controlled Assessment (CA)

You should be aware of the following:

- You will have a specified period of time (see times above) in class in which to write your response.
- You will write your response under exam conditions – there will be no teacher support and you will be closely supervised.
- You can have a **plain copy of the text** that you are writing about but you will **not** be allowed to bring in any notes to help you.
- You will not be allowed to take your work home.
- You only get **one** chance to do a CA Task.

What will you be asked to do in this CA?

You will write an essay in response to a question that you will have known in advance. The question that you will answer could be general such as:

> Analyse how the theme of love has been presented in a text you have studied.

Or, you could be asked to answer on a specific aspect of the text(s).

> Discuss the role of superstition in *Macbeth*.

In this case you would need to focus on particular incidents and characters within the text(s) in relation to this issue.

You will study the chosen text(s) and your teacher will give you the CA question(s) that you will be expected to answer. You should be given the question(s) well in advance of the actual Controlled Assessment(s) so that you have plenty of time to **plan** and **prepare** in class and at home.

Whilst your teacher will guide you through the planning process it is vital that you work on your own at home so that you achieve your full potential. You will only have one chance to complete this piece therefore being well prepared is key to a good response.

The Assessment Objective for this CA

Your Assessment Objective in this task(s) is testing your **Responses to Literature/Literary texts.** You are being assessed on your ability to:

i) Read and understand texts, selecting material appropriate to purpose, bringing together material from different sources and making comparisons and cross-references as appropriate.

ii) Develop and sustain interpretations of writers' ideas and perspectives.

iii) Explain and evaluate how writers use linguistic, grammatical, structural and presentational features to achieve effects and engage and influence the reader.

iv) Understand texts in their social, cultural and historical contexts. (This final objective is only prescribed for English but for those of you taking the English Language specification, any discussion of a text is likely to include some references to context, where relevant.)

How your work will be marked

There are two parts to this process. Your CA will initially be marked out of 25 by your teacher who will assess how well you have analysed the key features of the question in relation to the various elements of the Assessment Objective. This initial marking will then be moderated to ensure that the application of the mark scheme has resulted in a just award for every candidate. Occasionally it is necessary to adjust these scores to ensure everyone has been treated fairly.

The aims of the plan:

To think carefully about how you are going to begin. The introduction is very important – your whole essay should develop from here.

To select and order the main points that you are going to focus on in the main body of your essay. When you have gathered together these main points, create a logical order for them and think about how much detail each requires and what quotations (if any) you intend to use to support them. When selecting quotations remember that as you will have a clean copy of your text you will be credited for the selection of appropriate quotation but not for copying out big sections that merely act as padding!

To decide about how you are going to conclude. Avoid a conclusion that summarises/ repeats what's already been said. You might think about you own personal reaction to the issue you've been analysing and discussing.

Planning – the key to completing an effective CA

In class over a period of time your teacher will help you to plan and will provide feedback to you as you explore your ideas about the question. At home there are many things that you can do.

 Re-read the text(s) in your own time. This is the first step in preparing for this CA and it is essential if you are to have the depth of understanding that you need for success. Focus on this to begin with – without this detailed knowledge you cannot expect to do well. Reading the text(s) when you know the CA question(s) is particularly useful, as you will be reading the text(s) fully focused on what you will be writing about.

 Make notes as you read the text(s). This will obviously depend on the question posed. You may make a note of quotations linked directly to the theme(s) that you are focusing on – quotes on relevant characters, setting, plot and structure may be useful too or you may make notes on effective/significant language. Remember, don't copy out great lumps of text and keep your notes as brief as possible!

 Research what critics have to say. What do other people have to say about the text(s) or the theme(s) that you are focusing on? You can do this by using the internet sensibly or your school/local library. Reading other perspectives will give you some new ideas and will also challenge your own opinions. You may also find quotations from critics that you may use in your response(s).

 Plan your response carefully. Having completed your background work (remember that this will be a combination of what you are doing in school with your teacher and on your own at home), you can begin thinking about your plan. This plan is an absolutely essential piece of preparation for your CA.

 Practice! Practice! Practice! Remember that you will only get one chance to do this CA, therefore you would be well advised to practise responding, giving yourself the allotted time and writing a piece under CA conditions. It's essential that you know how much you can write in the time at your disposal – too little and you will have sold yourself short, too much and you will not finish and the piece will be hurried and increasingly errors will appear. Get used to working at the required speed!

 Look closely at the assessment criteria. Focusing on what will be used to mark your work will ensure that you are meeting all the targets that you should be! What mark would you give yourself if you were marking your work? Once you have marked your work, think about how you could improve before the actual CA.

Writing your answer: top tips to ensure success

 Know the elements/techniques associated with the genre that you are writing about – prose, poetry, drama – so that you know what you should be commenting on within your essay(s).

There are elements that are common to all three such as language and structure; however, in relation to:

- **prose** – focus on the particular elements associated with it as a genre such as **plot, setting and characterisation**
- **poetry** – recognise and understand the **poetic techniques** used such as rhyme, rhythm and imagery
- **drama** – consider focusing on **plot, setting, dialogue and characterisation** as these are some of the relevant aspects.

 Begin with a strong introduction. Your opening is crucial, as you want to take hold of the reader's attention. Aim to open in an original/thoughtful way. You could use a quotation from someone, a line from a song, a question, a proverb, an interesting fact or a short, strong statement to name just a few options. Remember whatever way you begin you must ensure that it is relevant. The 'attention grabber' must link with the theme and/or the question directly.

 Organise your ideas into strong points. Choose the points that you want to explore and organise them. Make sure that your points deal with all aspects of the question and are detailed. Organise these points into order of importance. Present your strongest argument first and your weakest one last.

 Make sure that you support your points with evidence. You will gain marks for using quotations to support the points that you make. The quotations that you use must be carefully chosen and should be brief. If you are quoting more than one line of a play or a poem, then use the line spacing and layout as it appears in the text. If you are quoting individual words and phrases simply use inverted commas within the sentence. You may also want to use quotations from critics that you have discovered during your preparation period to demonstrate your knowledge and understanding further. The important thing to remember with all quotations is that they should be linked with the point that you are making and you should provide an explanation. In other words, **P** (Point) **E** (Evidence) **E** (Explain).

 Make sure that you link back to the question. This does not mean that you keep repeating the question at the end of your paragraphs to show that you are answering it. At the end of each paragraph simply take a moment to read what you have written. Does what you have written connect with the question? Make sure that you are still on task and are not straying off the point. It is vital that you keep your essay focused at all times. Giving your paragraphs a topic sentence can also help you stay on task.

 Use connectives and discourse markers. Don't just present each argument as a separate, isolated paragraph. You will be credited for linking one paragraph to the next with: Moreover/On the other hand/In addition to name just a few. Also, you may want to use certain words to show that you are following the PEE structure. For example:

- **Point**: Firstly/to conclude/initially.
- **Evidence**: For example/for instance/this is shown when.
- **Explain**: It appears that/this suggests/we can conclude that.

Learn to use discourse markers and connectives before you do your CA so that they come naturally to you.

Ensure your spelling, punctuation and grammar are all sound. Make sure that you spell correctly those words that you use frequently (especially the names of characters in the piece of literature you are writing about!) but also aim to learn new words that will allow you to demonstrate that your vocabulary is extended. When it comes to punctuation try your best to use a range of punctuation including full stops, commas, colons, semi-colons, question marks, exclamation marks and dashes to name just a few types available to you. Effective punctuation will clarify what you are saying and will show that you are controlling the way that the reader reads your work. Make sure that you use paragraphs to structure your piece and ensure your grammar is accurate. Avoid abbreviations, pay particular attention to your use of tenses and make sure that you do not use text message language!

 Ensure that you end strongly. It is very important that you leave a lasting impression on the reader – this is why your conclusion is so important. Remember the 'attention grabbers' that you considered for the introduction? Why not use one of those to end your piece? You could also add a personal touch to the piece by commenting on how the text made you feel, your views on the theme discussed or how your opinion has changed as a result of studying the text. Your conclusion should round off the essay – therefore, you should not introduce another new point.

Check your understanding – Unit 4: Literary Study

1 I have an assured knowledge of the text(s)

2 I have organised how I am going to use my time in order to answer the task(s) effectively

3 I have practised under exam conditions in order to get up to CA speed

4 I understand the necessity of keeping the focus on the question I am going to answer

5 I understand how my plan will allow me to present a well organised and structured discussion

6 I have a clear understanding of my introduction and how my essay will begin and develop

7 I understand the need to support my discussion using **PEE**

8 I understand the need to demonstrate knowledge of the techniques that the writer has used and explain the impact that these choices have on the text

9 I have prepared so I can present a perceptive discussion

10 I have planned to engage the reader throughout but especially at the beginning and the end

11 I have worked to develop a competent use of spelling, punctuation and grammar

12 I understand how to vary my connectives for effect

13 I know how to use quotations briefly and effectively

Unit **4**

What you have to do

In English Language, this Task – **Writing Creatively** (Task 3) – is tested through Controlled Assessment and is worth 15 per cent of your final GCSE grade.

In English, these two Tasks – **Writing for Purpose** (Task 4 and 5) – are tested through Controlled Assessment and are worth 20 per cent of your final GCSE grade.

The **focus** of the Task(s) will be to explore and/or highlight an aspect of **one of three themes** specified annually by CCEA. You also need to note the following:

- In English Language you will have **2 hours** to plan and write your response – this time may be divided into more than one session.
- In English you will have a total of **3 hours** to complete the two pieces – this time may be divided into more than one session.
- If you complete the work over more than one session, this will be collected and stored after each session. You will not be allowed access to your work between sessions.
- You are responsible for planning the work, not your teacher, but your teacher will provide you with appropriate levels of guidance and support.
- There will be a high level of supervision when you are writing your response – your teacher will not be able to help you and you will have no access to a dictionary, a thesaurus, the internet or a spellcheck computer programme.
- You will not be allowed to take your work home.
- At the end of the supervision period, you will not be allowed to make any further changes to your piece of writing.
- You only get one chance to do a Controlled Assessment (CA) piece.

How your work will be marked

There is a rigorous process involved to ensure you get the mark you deserve.

- Your teacher will mark your piece out of **30 marks** using the Assessment Criteria provided by CCEA.
- Up to **20 marks** will be awarded for how well you have developed the piece in terms of engaging your audience with a range of language and structural effects.

- Up to **10 marks** will be awarded for your control in punctuation, grammar and spelling.
- Every school is required to carry out Internal Standardisation of CA Tasks in order to make sure that each teacher has applied the Assessment Criteria fairly and consistently.
- As a further check, CCEA will carry out a moderation process when all schools will be required to send in a random sample of their candidates' work. Sometimes it is necessary to adjust marks to bring the marking into line with CCEA's agreed standards.

The Assessment Objectives

For English and English Language, it is important to remind yourself of what is expected of you in this CA writing Task(s):

i) Write clearly, effectively and imaginatively to engage the reader.

ii) Use a form and select vocabulary that matches purpose and audience.

iii) Organise ideas/information logically into sentences and paragraphs.

iv) Make use of language and structural features for effect.

v) Use a range of sentence structures as well as punctuate and spell accurately.

In English Language you will be producing a piece of creative writing.

If you are taking English you will have two pieces to produce. You will be required to write in two different forms for two different audiences, informing, persuading or engaging. One piece has to be 'transactional' writing (e.g. a newspaper article outlining the pressures facing teenagers today). The other may be 'creative'.

What you have to do to succeed

- Choose an appropriate **form** for your writing which will allow you an effective way of exploring your chosen **theme**.
- In theory you can choose any form you want. In reality you'll succeed at what you do best! Experiment and practise different forms and techniques in the preparation period leading up to your CA supervised session(s).
- **Form**, **purpose** and **audience** are closely linked, but think carefully about issues such as the age range and gender of your target audience as this will establish the **style** you should adopt.
- Make the most of the **key stylistic features** for your selected form to **engage** your audience.
- Think about the **language** you are going to use — carefully select particular words such as adjectives and verbs for maximum impact.
- **Structure** your work effectively to give coherence to your piece — e.g. by giving careful thought into how the plot of a narrative should unfold. Also, don't forget to paragraph your work.
- Use a **variety of sentence forms** — to enliven your writing, to create a particular atmosphere or to emphasise a point.
- Produce as **accurate** a piece of writing as you can — leave time to check for mistakes.

Planning – the key to completing an effective CA

This is the key to a successful outcome. You will have plenty of time to prepare for this Task(s) so there is really no reason to go into the formal CA period without a clearly defined strategy!

 Decide what form your writing should take.
Let's take the theme of **adventure** as an example. This theme could be highlighted using a variety of forms: an adventure story for children; a travel piece for a magazine about adventure holidays or a review of an adventure film.

 Plan a gripping/challenging opening and conclusion.

Review this checklist of possible tactics for openings and endings:

Openings:

- the use of humour to entertain
- start with a dramatic moment
- internal monologue
- using dialogue between characters
- an intriguing situation or statement
- descriptive writing: for example, about a character or place
- an emotive opening: for example, to provoke shock or fear
- use a first person narrator for direct appeal
- a provocative/emphatic statement
- using persuasive devices such as questions, repetition or a list
- a personal anecdote or real-life scenario
- use an apt quotation
- effective use of factual material.

Endings:

- a rhetorical device such as a question which challenges the reader's views
- a 'cliff hanger' ending which leaves the reader wondering what happens next
- leave the reader with a strong message to consider
- an unexpected twist which takes the reader by surprise
- a 'happy ever after' or 'feel-good' ending
- an apt quotation which makes the reader think
- an emotive statement
- the use of a short sentence
- the use of a strong visual image
- an evocative description
- a direct appeal to the reader
- something a character says or thinks.

Plan to use techniques to sustain interest and to create the effects you're after.

Here are a range of narrative techniques you can use to create an engaging story:

- An interesting **plot** appropriate for the targeted age range.

- Varying the **pace** at which the story unfolds.

- Creating and developing **characters**.

- Using **dialogue** and **internal monologue** to bring characters to life.

- Using **setting** to create atmosphere.

- Hooking the reader with a gripping **opening**.

- Building up to a **dramatic moment**.

- Crafting an inventive/original **conclusion**.

- Using devices such as simile and metaphor to create **imagery**.

- Appealing to the reader's **senses** to add vividness and increase the reader's involvement in the story.

- Using a **variety of sentence forms** to add interest and create effects.

- **Punctuate for effect** – for example, to indicate a dramatic moment or to convey tension in a conversation.

- Use **language** effectively for descriptive touches for example, or to create suspense!

You need to have it in mind to use a range of these strategies intentionally so go into the supervised period with these at your fingertips. Be properly prepared!

It is important to use techniques that are appropriate for the form you have chosen in order to achieve your intended purpose with your target audience.

This section concludes with a couple of mnemonics that summarise this neatly.

Check your understanding – Unit 4: Writing Creatively/Writing for Purpose

Provoke an emotional response from your audience ☐	**C**reate interest from the start ☐
Express strong opinions – in an appropriate manner! ☐	**R**emember to choose words carefully ☐
Relate personal anecdotes – get the reader to empathise with you ☐	**E**ngage your audience throughout ☐
Sustain interest – present well supported arguments ☐	**A**ccuracy – always check your work ☐
Use inclusive language – 'we' and 'everyone knows' ☐	**T**echniques – use for impact ☐
Appeal directly to your reader – e.g. challenging with a rhetorical question ☐	**I**nclude a great ending ☐
Direct your reader's response, use imperatives – get them on your side! ☐	**V**ariety of sentences ☐
Engage the reader – use a lively style ☐	**E**ffects, effects, effects! ☐

This CA is your chance to create an original piece of writing that is uniquely a product of your imagination, thoughts, personality and ingenuity.

In order to take the opportunity to score well in this Task, remember the following:

    P – Purpose

    A – Audience

    F – Form

    T – Techniques

One final thought – all the advice about writing can be summarised into three short words:

PLAN **WRITE** **CHECK**

Common mistakes and top exam tips

Here are a series of straightforward errors and mix-ups that students make in exams time and time again.

It is likely that you will be guilty of some of these errors – if you are to maximise your performance, then you need to get to grips with these and sort them out. This section should help you – tick them off as you go!

Getting to grips: words that are frequently confused

a lot	accidentally	are/our
believe	chose/choose	definitely
difference	embarrass	environment
especially	excitement	exclamation mark
exercise	form/from	happened
humour/humorous	information	interesting
lose/loose	maybe	necessary
of/off	opinion	opportunity
perform	principal/principle	professional
quite/quiet	receive	right/write
statistics	successful	surely
their/there/they're	though/thought	threw/through
to/too/two	where/were/we're	your/you're

Practical session for improvement

See if you can you find the 20 errors in the following piece.

> Were have yous been? Your missing all the excitment, its been quiet a morning. Are principle fell write threw the greenhouse window, I was their when it happend. He was so embarassed, his proffessional pride was definately dented. It was mayby to much for him because his wig come lose as well!

Getting to grips: grammar

Here are the errors that cause examiners the most alarm – again these are relatively easy to sort out.

- Writing 'youse', 'you's', 'use' or the text speak version 'u' instead of 'you'. The plural of 'you' is 'you' – there is **only** 'YOU' – every other version is wrong!
- Inaccuracy in the use of the following: *due to/because of; amount/number; less/fewer.*

- Confusing did/done. Remember: '*I did* my homework last night' and '*I have (I've) done* you a favour':
- Confusing saw/seen. Remember: '*I saw* you in the canteen' and 'Now *I have (I've) seen* everything!'
- Writing *could of* or *should of* is incorrect; the correct form is: *could have (could've)* and *should have (should've).*

Getting to grips: punctuation

Poorly punctuated work is confusing to read. There are some basic rules you must follow to communicate clearly what you mean:

- Every sentence needs to begin with a capital letter and end with an end stop: full stop, question mark or an exclamation mark.
- The personal pronoun 'I' must be written as a capital letter.
- Only use apostrophes when letters have been left out as in '*don't*' (do not) or to show ownership as in '*the students's exercise book*' (the exercise book belonging to one student). Don't use apostrophes with plural words as in '*the girls are outside*'.
- Use inverted commas (speech marks) to indicate quotations, the title of a text or direct speech.
- Commas tell the reader when to pause and are not to be confused with full stops.

Punctuation can also enliven your written work as it indicates your feelings and conveys a sense of your personality to the reader. Make sure you use a range of punctuation to achieve this:

- Indicate a sense of outrage or frustration, for example, with several questions in succession.
- Signal strong emotion with exclamatory sentences – a sentence with double exclamations can be used as a humorous touch!!
- Dashes, hyphens and brackets can also be used to good effect to convey opinions and to entertain the reader.
- Colons and semi-colons are useful to: introduce lists and quotations; separating items in a list; joining two or more sentences about the same topic together.

Getting to grips: sentence structure

Of course sentence structure is something to which you should pay particular attention. In English there are three main types of sentence structure that you need to understand. These are:

a) the **simple** sentence

b) the **compound** sentence

c) the **complex** sentence.

You can use your knowledge of these in all sections of the exam because once you understand them you will be able to:

- identify the different types of sentence and so explain why they have been used in a particular situation in **reading**
- make use of their different qualities in your **writing**
- use their qualities in some of your **Speaking and Listening** scenarios.

The functions of different sentences

A writer will use a range of sentence structures to give work variety and ensure that it doesn't become boring. In general a **shorter sentence will create greater dramatic effect** – it forces you to pause and think about what has just been said. On the other hand, **longer sentences help a piece to flow** more and, with less use of punctuation, enable the pace of the piece to increase.

The simple sentence

The most basic type of sentence is the **simple sentence**, which contains only one clause. A simple sentence can be as short as one word: *Go!*

All of the following are simple sentences, because each contains only one clause:

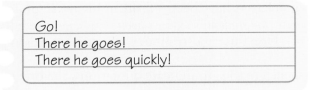

Simple sentences are used to grab the reader's attention and are particularly effective when they follow a longer sentence as they stand out.

The compound sentence

A **compound sentence** consists of two or more **independent clauses** (or simple sentences) joined by a conjunction like 'and', 'but' and 'or':

For example, a simple sentence: The shops in New York are fantastic.

For example, a compound sentence: The shops in New York are fantastic but they are very crowded.

A compound sentence is most effective when you use it to create a sense of **balance** or **contrast** between two (or more) equally important pieces of information: Emma is a great singer but Anna has greater acting ability.

The complex sentence

A **complex sentence** contains one independent clause and at least one dependent clause. Unlike a compound sentence, however, a complex sentence contains clauses which are *not* equal. Consider the following examples of sentences:

A simple sentence – this example has two simple sentences: My best friend asked me to go shopping. I do not want to go.

A compound sentence: My best friend asked me to go shopping, but I do not want to go.

This example has a conjunction joining the two parts together. The two parts could stand independently and still make sense. They are equal.

A complex sentence: Although my best friend asked me to go shopping, I don't want to.

The word 'Although' has changed the sentence. 'Although my best friend asked me to go shopping,' has become incomplete. It does not stand independently.

A complex sentence is very different from a simple sentence or a compound sentence because it makes clear which ideas are most important. When 'Although' is placed at the beginning of the first clause, it is clear that the shopping invitation is less important than the fact that you do not want to go.

Here are the names of some other types of sentences – you already use them on a regular basis:

Declarative sentence – makes a statement. A declarative sentence ends with a full stop: The party will be at my house.

Interrogative sentence – asks a question, so therefore ends with a question mark: Where did you find the boy?

Exclamatory sentence – shows strong emotion therefore ends with an exclamation mark: That is absolutely disgusting!

Imperative sentence – gives a command: Close the window.

Practical session for improvement

For each of the following, identify the sentence type. The first one has been done for you.

1 Why did you do that?   Interrogative
2 Ask Jim for that book.
3 You are scaring me!
4 My friend asked me to go to the cinema, however I already had plans.
5 I have a hospital appointment tomorrow.
6 Jim, pass the salt.
7 Your cake is lovely but my mum's is even better.

Getting to grips: using quotations

As in any piece of assessed English, whether in an exam or a Controlled Assessment (CA) Task, quotations should:

- be **brief**
- **illustrate** the point you are making
- be **fluently embedded** into your commentary.

Here are some practical examples:

- Do **not** use a quotation **simply to repeat a point** you have already made. Boxer is a hard-working animal. He says: 'I will work harder.' Instead, look at how this quotation could be integrated into an informed personal comment: Boxer steadfastly believes that sustained physical effort is the key to the success of Animalism and this is expressed in his often-repeated personal saying, 'I will work harder.'
- Use quotations to **illustrate** points you are making. The sarcastic tone injects humour into the piece: 'the average American gets through 300 gigajoules. And 40 burgers.'

- Use a quotation **to make a point** (or points!) for you: *George concisely sums up the main features of Lennie when he introduces him to Slim: 'Hell of a nice fella, but he ain't bright.'*
- Make sure the quotation is **fluently embedded** into the sentence: *His campaign slogan summarised his character and belief perfectly: 'Yes we can!'*
- Quotations should be **brief**, **meaningful** and **relevant**: *Atticus does not condemn the men who come with the intention of lynching Tom Robinson; they are his neighbours and even though they are behaving like 'a gang of wild animals', he has the strong conviction that 'they're still human' underneath.*

Top exam tips

1 **Take time to 'unpack' the examination tasks**. Knowing what is required of you is the first step to a successful response!

2 Underline or highlight important words to help **keep your answers focused**.

3 **Make sure you carefully read what you have to do.** Basic mistakes are often made when this is not done properly:

- take heed of the **basic guidance** on the front cover of the exam paper
- **take sufficient time to read each task thoroughly**, 'unpacking' them carefully. This helps to avoid hasty and unplanned responses
- **underline or highlight** supporting evidence in the stimulus material – **you are entitled to annotate your copy of the exam paper!**

4 **Use the PEE and PEA strategies as the basis of your answers:**

- When writing essays, **PEE** is an excellent way to structure your ideas and opinions. It also helps you to organise your written work into paragraphs:
  P-Point: state clearly what point/idea/opinion you wish to express.
  E-Evidence: give examples to support the point you are making. This could be in the form of personal anecdotes, real-life examples, quotes or factual information.
  E-Explain: add further comment to reinforce your viewpoint.
- When responding to reading tasks, **PEA** forms the basis of a focused response and ensures an analytical approach:
  P-Point: state clearly what conclusion/inference you wish to make.
  E-Evidence: offer supporting textual evidence.
  A-Analysis: refer back to the demands of the task, making clear how the point and evidence given show your understanding.

5 **Avoid being boring when you are writing!**

You wouldn't choose to read a boring book so why present the examiner with dull and uninspiring stuff? Try to capture your reader's attention right from the start.

6   **Plan your responses** – this is another must!

- You have already been advised to take 5–10 minutes to create a short plan for a writing task. **Jot down a checklist of ideas/opinions/information to include in your piece of writing**. This helps ensure you have a clear structure for your thoughts. In particular, **it is vital to think through how you intend to start and conclude the written piece**.

- In response to reading tasks, it is important to plan – **draw a quick spider diagram, write down key words and identify textual evidence** you are going to use.

7   **Write as accurately and clearly as possible**.

- Don't regurgitate an old essay, trying to make it fit a different task – **take a fresh approach**.

- Think carefully about what it is you want to get across (the **purpose**) and who you are writing for (the **reader/audience**).

- **Always proof-read**. Check your work makes sense and cross out/re-write sentences that are unclear or unnecessary. If you notice any spelling mistakes, correct them.

8   **Using abbreviations and bullet points**. Write in complete sentences to present your ideas – unless you are short of time!

9   **Take note of the mark allocations for each task**. This is important as it is another means to guide you as to how long to spend on individual tasks.

Practical session for improvement

Replace the following very ordinary opening by creating an interesting one which would engage and entertain the reader:

> In this essay I am going to write about school uniform. This is an important subject and people have different opinions. I am going to give arguments for and then arguments against then I am going to come to a conclusion at the end.

Take the above advice seriously – it will help secure you the best possible mark and could improve your final grade!

Check your understanding – Reading

1 I have a more secure understanding of sentence types and their functions ☐

2 I know how to use quotations effectively and efficiently ☐

3 I understand how to unpack questions ☐

4 I recognise key words in questions ☐

5 I know how to use **PEA** when answering reading questions ☐

6 I use the key words so that my answers are focused and analytical in approach ☐

7 I recognise the purpose and can identify the target audience in different types of texts ☐

8 I understand that language varies according to audience ☐

9 I can identify tone/tonal shifts and how this is meant to affect the reader's response ☐

10 I can explain how writers use linguistic and presentational devices to sustain the reader's interest in multi-modal texts ☐

11 I can compare and contrast how language is used in multi-modal texts ☐

12 I can explain how writers use linguistic, grammatical and structural features to influence the reader in non-fiction texts ☐

Check your understanding – Writing

1 I've sorted out basic spelling, punctuation and grammar issues that I had ☐

2 I can use different writing forms and understand the importance of audience and purpose in selecting appropriate vocabulary ☐

3 I understand the importance of original and engaging openings and strong conclusions ☐

4 I use different kinds of sentences for effect such as: exclamatory sentences, questions and short sentences ☐

5 I remember to use linkers so that my writing is structured clearly ☐

6 I remember to use discursive markers such as 'surely' and 'on the other hand' ☐

7 My writing is flexible and lively in style, showing enthusiasm as appropriate ☐

8 I think about what words I am going to use for maximum effect ☐

9 I use a range of punctuation to liven up my writing and to help emphasise my opinions, feelings and emotions ☐

10 I organise my ideas in a coherent manner ☐

11 I can use humour when appropriate ☐

12 I can express my own, independent views appropriately ☐

13 My written work is as accurate as possible (I leave time to check over my writing) as I am aware of the mistakes I can make and am taking responsibility in this area ☐

Unit 1

Sample questions and mark schemes

Unit 1 Foundation Tier (90 minutes)

Section A: Personal Writing

Up to **16 marks** are available for an interesting and organised piece of writing.

Up to **8 marks** are available for the use of a range of sentence structures and correct spelling, punctuation and grammar.

Task 1

Write about your best friend.

In your answer you might want to:

- describe this friend

- explain how you feel about your friend and the reasons for your choice. **[24]**

Planning your answer. . .

It is suggested that you organise your time like this:

- **5–10 minutes** planning your answer
- **25–30 minutes** writing your response
- **5 minutes** checking over your writing.

Section B: Reading Multi-Modal Texts

The websites for Volvic and Gatorade are designed to promote their drinks products. (See page 74.)

Task 2

Compare and contrast how **presentational devices** are used in **both** websites to make the products appealing to an audience.

Analyse the use of **images, colour** and the **layout**. **[9]**

Task 3

Compare and contrast how **language** has been used in **both** websites to persuade you to buy these products. **[15]**

Planning your answers. . .

It is suggested that you organise your time like this:

- **10–15 minutes** carefully studying both texts
- **25–30 minutes** writing your responses to the tasks
- **5 minutes** checking that your answers are clearly expressed.

The opening page of the **Gatorade** website.

The Volvic website. Jonny Wilkinson is a famous rugby player.

Unit 1 Higher Tier (90 minutes)

Section A: Personal Writing

Up to **16 marks** are available for an interesting and organised piece of writing.

Up to **8 marks** are available for the use of a range of sentence structures and correct spelling, punctuation and grammar.

Task 1

Write about what you hope for in the next ten years of your life. **[24]**

Section B: Reading Multi-Modal Texts

On pages 76 and 77 are the inside spreads taken from two brochures promoting activity centres (the Quorn Hall International Centre and Todd's Leap). The interior of these brochures are designed to inform the reader and promote these centres.

Task 2

Compare and contrast how **presentational devices** are used in **both** to make these centres appeal to the reader.

Analyse the use of **images, colour** and the **layout**. **[9]**

Task 3

Compare and contrast how **language** has been used in **both** centre page spreads to inform the reader and promote what each centre has to offer. **[15]**

Quorn Hall International Centre

ACTIVITIES

Quorn Hall International Centre can offer supported and unsupported activities. Supported activities can be arranged in conjunction with fully qualified teachers / instructors based on site and at nearby Beaumanor Education Centre. These include canoeing, climbing, walking, archery, team building, orienteering and other outdoor activities. Beaumanor Park also offers a range of field study and day activities for groups visiting Quorn Hall.

LOCATION

Quorn Hall is located in the village of Quorn about 2 miles from Loughborough. It is easily reached by British Rail to Loughborough or by road from the A6 and the M1.

SITUATION

Quorn Hall stands in large grounds and is surrounded by lawns and trees. Adjacent to the Hall is the River Soar. There is ample space to relax and enjoy the scenery or to use the lawned areas around the Hall for recreational activities.

HISTORY

The original Hall was built as a family home in the late 17th century. From 1753 to 1903 it was the home of the Quorn Hunt. It was eventually purchased by Leicestershire County Council and became the International Centre in 1977.

CATERING

Quorn Hall catering is a speciality, whether breakfast, lunch or evening meal. For groups wishing to return later than the normal evening meal time a cold meal can be provided by prior arrangement. Groups are asked to help with some of the cleaning up duties.

USAGE

Quorn Hall caters primarily for student groups from those areas of Europe with which Leicestershire has educational links and also Leicestershire schools, colleges and youth groups. Conference facilities are also available.

ACCOMMODATION

Quorn Hall has accommodation for 120 people arranged in dormitories for 4-10, with 8 twin bedded en-suite rooms. There is a twin bedded room with an en-suite bathroom on the ground floor suitable for visitors with disabilities.

FACILITIES

Quorn Hall offers warm and comfortable accommodation. Facilities include several study rooms and a games room. Various items of audio-visual and sports equipment are available for use by resident groups.

Educational Activities

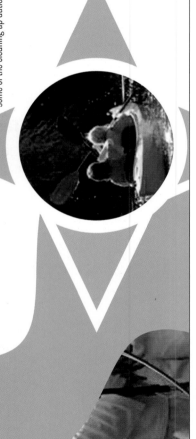

NOW, ARE YOU READY FOR SOME SERIOUS FUN?

Todds Leap outdoor activity centre

Todds Leap offers an exciting mixture of adventure and team building activities for groups and individuals. Todds Leap for an experience you'll never, ever, forget!!!!

GAME ON!!!

- Clay Pigeon Shooting
- Quad Bike Riding
- Hill Rally Stage
- Off Road Driving

- Super Slide
- Zip Line
- Paintball
- Rodeo Bull

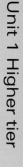

ADVENTURE ACTIVITIES

ARCHERY
If you fancy yourself as a Robin Hood or William Tell, then our instructors will teach you how to send the arrows flying and hopefully hit that all elusive GOLD!

BLINDFOLD DRIVING
Blindfold Land Rover Driving at Todds Leap is exactly what it says on the tin, driving a Land Rover blindfolded! Your vehicle for the day will be a Land Rover Troop Carrier and your destination is around our course safely without knocking down any obstacles in your way. You won't be under guidance of any instructor, you will be totally dependant on your passengers in the back seat for directions. Can you really trust them?

JCB DRIVING
Take turns to compete against each other moving gravel into a series of barrels and moving obstacles. Alternatively you can just get carried away digging holes, which oddly for some can be a 'hole' lot of fun!

CLIMBING WALL
The outdoor Climbing Wall simulates a variety of rock formations to provide participants with a fun & challenging activity. The Wall is set with a variety of routes to suit all ages and abilities with full instruction by qualified and experienced instructors.

ZIPLINE
Prepare for highflying fun as you harness up and glide through the air on this thrilling, action packed Zip Line adventure. Travel half a mile through the heart of Todds Leap, from our highest point to our base at the clubhouse, with only gravity for brakes.

RODEO BULL
The classic Rodeo Bull is always a winner. The ride provides as much amusement for the spectators as it does for the rider. Our Rodeo will buck, spin and turn in its efforts to get you off, landing you on the safety of the inflatable bed that surrounds it. Suitable for 16+.

SUPER SLIDE
The giant Super Slide showcases itself at the face of the centre, standing 100ft in height, this magnificent landmark is the first thing you will see as you arrive at Todds Leap. One of Europe's largest inflatable slides, this over sized toy guarantees you the slide of your life! Suitable for 14+.

AND FOR THE FINALE... HILL RALLY STAGE

HILL RALLY STAGE EVENT
Finish off the day on a real high with the Hill Rally Stage, completely exclusive to the centre. No day at Todds Leap is complete without this high adrenaline activity. Also known as our white knuckle run, you will be strapped into a specially prepared passenger Land Rover, and your chauffeur for the day will take you across the off road course at a competitive race speed time. All safety equipment and professional instruction is provided so you are in good (safe) hands!

All of the following mark schemes have been cut back slightly, but in terms of the content and levels of competence descriptors, these are exactly what would be used to assess these tasks. For your revision functions these mark schemes have two purposes: to allow you to assess the overall standard of your own work; and to enable you to work out what you have done well and what other points you could have included so that you can improve your next performance!

Foundation Unit 1 Section A

Task 1: Personal Writing 1st assessment (maximum of 16 marks)

Response time: 45 minutes.

Write about your best friend. Describe this friend/explain how you feel about your friend and the reasons for your choice.

The task-specific checklist below outlines the skills associated with Writing AOs (i) and (ii) (see page 14) that candidates at all competence levels may be expected to attempt to employ in their responses.

Communicate clearly and effectively and imaginatively, demonstrating:
- a handling of the topic in such a way as to attempt to positively develop the reader's interest
- use of a style that endeavours to build a positive relationship with the target audience
- possible use of anecdotes/humour to engage the audience.

Adapting form and vocabulary to task and purpose in ways that engage the reader, demonstrating:
- an awareness of the examiner as audience
- a use of tone that is meant to engage and sustain the audience's attention
- use of a straightforward vocabulary that is in keeping with the task and audience and that, occasionally, may enliven the writing.

Organise information and ideas into structured, sequenced sentences, paragraphs and whole texts, demonstrating:
- a sense of progression – the reader being taken through the writer's experience
- an awareness of opening and closing paragraphs
- some use of topic sentences for different paragraphs
- development that uses organisation in an attempt to hold the audience's interest.

Use a variety of linguistic and structural features for coherence, demonstrating:
- some variety of sentence length for effect
- occasional use of connectives to give coherence to paragraphing
- the use of rhetorical devices – questions, exclamation marks, the rule of three, etc.

Competence level 1 [1–4]
Characterised by:
- general, rather superficial development
- an unconvincing grasp of purpose and audience
- some attempt at simple structure using a rudimentary style.

Competence level 2 [5–8]
Characterised by:
- a simple development, relating content in an elementary manner
- a broad sense of purpose and/or audience that may be sustained
- a basic structure and an elementary style.

Competence level 3 [9–12]
Characterised by:
- an uncomplicated development, relating the content in a deliberate fashion
- a general sense of purpose and audience
- a logical structure and a straightforward style.

Competence level 4 [13–16]
Characterised by:
- a generally effective development that maintains the reader's interest
- a recognition of purpose and audience
- a clear use of structure and an increasingly fluent style.

Task 1: Personal Writing 2nd assessment (maximum of 8 marks)

This task-specific checklist outlines the skills associated with Writing AO (iii) (see page 14) that candidates at all competence levels may be expected to attempt to employ in their responses.

The range of sentence structures used and their effectiveness:

- The wider the control that a candidate shows in the use of sentence structures, the greater is his/her ability to sustain interest and establish a relationship with the audience/examiner. The more competent and varied that use of sentence structure is, the higher will be the mark awarded.

The use made of accurate punctuation and spelling:

- A central part of sentence structure is the control that comes from the accurate use of various forms of punctuation. Here too there is scope for variety that can help to engage the audience/examiner. The greater the range of punctuation appropriately used, the higher will be the reward.
- Accuracy in spelling, viewed on its own, could be misleading; it needs to be viewed along with the range and precision of the vocabulary that a candidate draws upon. A limited and dull vocabulary spelt with absolute accuracy is unlikely to capture the attention of the audience/examiner. Credit attempts to use vocabulary ambitiously where the word may not always be accurately spelt but has been chosen with care.

Competence level 1 [1–2]
Characterised by:

- little control of sentence structuring – instead, simple connectives used to link ideas; verbs often repeated
- occasional use of full stops and commas tends to be the limit of punctuation
- some accuracy in the spelling of simple words
- the range of vocabulary is narrow.

Competence level 2 [3–4]
Characterised by:

- a use of basic sentence structuring that offers little variation in construction or length
- generally correct use of full stops and the use of some other forms of punctuation
- basic vocabulary is usually spelt accurately
- a limited vocabulary.

Competence level 3 [5–6]
Characterised by:

- a controlled use of straightforward sentence structuring – there will be evidence of some variety in sentence construction and length
- a generally secure use of basic punctuation to support structure
- generally accurate spelling of straightforward, regular vocabulary
- an uncomplicated vocabulary will be evident.

Competence level 4 [7–8]
Characterised by:

- increasingly sustained competence in the handling of a variety of sentence structures – occasionally these may be used for effect
- the basics of punctuation – full stops, commas, exclamation and question marks – used accurately, adding clarity to the work
- generally accurate spelling including some words with irregular patterns
- a greater precision in the use of a widening vocabulary.

Foundation Unit 1 Section B

Task 2: Reading Multi-Modal Texts (maximum of 9 marks)

Response time: 10 minutes

Compare and contrast how **presentational devices** are used in **both** websites to make the products appealing to an audience. Analyse the use of **images, colour** and the **layout**.

What follows is a task-specific checklist of evidence relating to the Assessment Objectives for Studying Written Language/Reading (see page 57). This contains examples of the types of material that candidates at all competence levels may be expected to include in their responses.

Competence level 1 [1–3]
Characterised by:
- a basic recognition that use has been made of presentational devices
- some reference to a few very obvious examples
- a very general linking of the examples of these devices to their purpose.

Competence level 2 [4–6]
Characterised by:
- an understanding of how some of these presentational devices support their purpose
- reference to a series of examples, some supported by straightforward comment
- some appropriate use of comparison and contrast at a straightforward level.

Competence level 3 [7–9]
Characterised by:
- a sound overall consideration of how some of the presentational devices generate specific outcomes
- a straightforward explanation and comparison of how these devices have been used
- the development of an appropriate interpretation of the stimulus through an uncomplicated drawing together of mainly appropriate evidence from both sources.

The use made of images and colour:

- Given the highly visual nature both front website opening pages, they follow very different agendas: Gatorade create a brooding, dramatic mood for their product whilst Volvic appeal to their readers by generating a much more friendly and inviting atmosphere. This is reflected in the colours chosen by each company: Gatorade uses black and grey, serious and formal colours; whereas Volvic has a range of bright colours (green, blue, yellow) to reflect its message to get involved and accept this fun challenge.
- Volvic use a background that is a shot of clear blue, swirling water taken apparently from in and under surface level. This clearly fits in with their desired image and message of a pure, healthy product. This 'purity concept' is further reinforced by the eco-friendly green background that is broken up into varying sections. By contrast, Gatorade's matt grey-black background creates a striking backdrop to their three featured products that are lit in such a way as to three-dimensionally reflect their lighting.
- The Gatorade colouring also serves to highlight the bold white font in 'G SERIES' and 'BEFORE/DURING/AFTER'. Volvic also use a highly visible yellow to highlight some of their text.
- Gatorade place their three products at the centre of an uncluttered webpage, whereas Volvic's focus seems to be mainly on a challenge built around their main image of Jonny Wilkinson. However, some product examples, namely their fruit-flavoured water, are promoted.
- Both companies use photographs on their webpages. Volvic has an additional photograph of Jonny Wilkinson actually drinking the product. Gatorade, however, present photographs of sportsmen actually drinking the product.
- Volvic could be described as a 'busier' webpage:
  - The recycling logos and the image of the smiling young African and map of Africa suggest they are keen to promote themselves as a company that cares and that they are making a positive difference in Third World countries.
  - An image of a volcano demonstrates the process of the natural filtering of their water. This image reflects the volcano image in Volvic's logo.
  - They use a comic image of a bottle on wheels to inform the reader of their delivery service.

The layout:

- Both are webpages as is evident from the use of links to other sections as well as embedded sound and vision clips – these have a practical impact on the design and layout. The informal approach by Volvic is reflected in the irregular, 'hand-drawn' sections which contrasts with the regimented and very symmetrical layout used by Gatorade.
- Gatorade is less cluttered or busy than its counterpart and as a result has possibly more visual impact than Volvic. It might be noted that the large block of uppercase text, however, is at odds with this.
- The role of a logo is much more prominent in the Gatorade page where it is employed at every opportunity, whereas Volvic only seriously present their logo once.
- The weblinks in the Gatorade webpage are clearly demarcated from the rest of the text on the left-hand side and top right, whereas, the weblinks in the Volvic webpage are embedded throughout the text. Gatorade has more formal buttons as links rather than the informal hand-drawn arrows used by Volvic.

Foundation Unit 1 Section B

Task 3: Reading Multi-Modal Texts (maximum of 15 marks)

Response time: 20 minutes

Compare and contrast how **language** has been used in **both** websites to persuade you to buy these products.

What follows is a task specific checklist of evidence relating to the Assessment Objectives for Studying Written Language/Reading (see page 57). This contains examples of the types of material that candidates at all competence levels may be expected to include in their responses.

How language has been used to promote these two products:

- The name 'G Series' makes the product sound technical/scientific implying an advantage is to be had by taking this drink; the name 'Volvic' has similar connotations, suggesting it is a drink with the power of a volcano.

- Gatorade uses the words 'BEFORE/DURING/AFTER' to promote these three products – the drinks are to 'fuel … athletes and active people.' Everyone would all like to consider themselves to be 'athletic' or at the very least 'active' people going places and doing things – so drinking these products will help to support a positive, flattering self-image.

- Volvic are building their campaign by using a different strategy. They are issuing a challenge – 'Drink 1.5l every day for 14 days' – which we are told elsewhere 'hydrates your body and mind' which will 'help you feel your best.'

- Gatorade's angle is much more technical: 'a scientifically proven blend of carbohydrates and key electrolytes'; whereas Volvic take a different approach by relying on our sense of curiosity: 'What gives Volvic its volcanicity?'/'THANK YOU Find out how you are helping make a difference.' Volvic's language is also more informal: 'What we're up to'/'It's a doddle.'/'Loads of people'.

- Gatorade's tone is aspirational/competitive: 'Be fueled to achieve your best every step of the way'/'to help athletes … refuel and push through'; whereas Volvic are taking a less formal, more environmental approach: 'Reducing our impact'/'What we're up to'. Both make very positive claims about their products. According to Gatorade one of their products is: 'the first protein and carbohydrate beverage with the consistency of a thirst quencher'. Volvic are also self-congratulatory, if rather less dramatic, in their claim: 'It's tough to beat Volvic plain, but with a Touch of Fruit we've come close!'

- Volvic's heading 'Join the Challenge' is a direct address, personally inviting the reader to take part. Volvic also uses a question to directly address and involve the reader – 'What's in it for you?' – and directly thanks the reader for helping make a difference: 'Thank You'. Gatorade also takes a direct and emphatic approach with the reader using the imperative: 'Be fuelled'/'Get technical'/'Learn more'.

Competence level 1 [1–5]
Characterised by:
- some basic sense of how language has been employed
- reference to a few obvious examples
- a very general linking of the examples of these devices to their purposes.

Competence level 2 [6–10]
Characterised by:
- an understanding of how some of these language effects can be employed to present information/generate excitement
- reference to a series of examples, some of which will be supported by straightforward comment
- some appropriate use of comparison and contrast at a straightforward level.

Competence level 3 [11–15]
Characterised by:
- a sound overall consideration of how some of the language strategies achieve their effects
- a straightforward explanation and comparison of how these effects have been used to support the purpose of each piece
- the development of an appropriate interpretation of the stimulus materials through an uncomplicated drawing together of mainly appropriate supporting evidence from both sources.

Higher Unit 1 Section A

Task 1: Personal Writing 1st assessment (maximum of 16 marks)

Response time: 45 minutes

Write about what you hope for in the next ten years of your life.

This task-specific checklist outlines the skills associated with Writing AOs (i) and (ii) (see page 14) that candidates at all competence levels may be expected to employ in their responses.

Communicate clearly and effectively and imaginatively, demonstrating:

- a handling of the topic in such a way as to positively develop the reader's interest
- use of a style that builds a positive relationship with the target audience
- possible use of anecdotes/humour to enliven the writing and so engage the audience.

Adapt form and vocabulary to task and purpose in ways that engage the reader, demonstrating:

- a conscious awareness of the examiner as audience
- a use of tone that is designed to engage and sustain the audience's attention
- use of vocabulary that is in keeping with the task and audience to enhance, enrich and enliven the writing.

Organise information and ideas into structured, sequenced sentences, paragraphs and whole texts demonstrating:

- a sense of logical progression – the reader being led through the writer's experience
- the use of opening and closing paragraphs
- the use of topic sentences for different paragraphs
- development that uses conscious organisation to sustain the audience's interest.

Use a variety of linguistic and structural features for cohesion and coherence demonstrating:

- a conscious varying of sentence length for effect
- the use of connectives to give coherence to paragraphing
- the use of rhetorical devices such as questions, exclamation marks, the rule of three, hyperbole, etc., to develop interest and a rapport with the audience.

Competence level 1 [1–4]
Characterised by:

- an uncomplicated development, relating the content in a deliberate fashion
- a general sense of purpose and audience
- a logical structure and a straightforward style.

Competence level 2 [5–8]
Characterised by:

- a generally effective development that maintains the reader's interest
- a recognition of purpose and audience
- a clear use of structure and an increasingly fluent style.

Competence level 3 [9–12]
Characterised by:

- a competent development that clearly interests the reader
- a confident awareness of purpose and audience
- proficiently structured writing including evidence of a developing, lively style.

Competence level 4 [13–16]
Characterised by:

- a poised and sophisticated development that commands the reader's attention throughout
- a positive rapport with the audience
- assured competence in terms of structure underpinned by a confident style.

Task 1: Personal writing 2nd assessment (maximum of 8 marks)

This task-specific checklist outlines the skills associated with Writing AO (iii) (see page 14) that candidates at all competence levels may be expected to attempt to employ in their responses. Credit the use of any other valid strategies used that are not mentioned below.

The range of sentence structures used and their effectiveness:

- The wider the range and greater the degree of originality and control used in sentence structuring, the more opportunity the candidate gives him/herself to establish a positive rapport with the reader.
- More assured and varied control and manipulation of sentence structuring demonstrates higher levels of competence and is to be rewarded accordingly.

The use made of accurate punctuation and spelling:

- Linked to the control of sentence structure is the control of a variety of appropriate forms of punctuation. Here too there is scope for creativity that can help to engage the examiner's interest. The greater the control and innovation in the use of punctuation the higher will be the reward.
- Accuracy in spelling, in isolation, can be misleading; it needs to be viewed beside the range and precision of the vocabulary used. A limited and mundane vocabulary spelt with unerring accuracy is unlikely to capture the attention. Credit ambitious use of vocabulary where the word may not always be accurately spelt but has been chosen with care to capture the essence of a situation.

Competence level 1 [1–2]
Characterised by:

- a controlled use of straightforward sentence structuring – there will be evidence of some variety in sentence construction and length
- a generally secure use of basic punctuation to support structure
- generally accurate spelling of straightforward, regular vocabulary
- an uncomplicated vocabulary will be evident.

Competence level 2 [3–4]
Characterised by:

- increasingly sustained competence in the handling of a variety of sentence structures – occasionally these may be used for effect
- the basics of punctuation – full stops, commas, exclamation and question marks – used accurately, adding clarity to the work
- generally accurate spelling including some words with irregular patterns
- a greater precision in the use of a widening vocabulary.

Competence level 3 [5–6]
Characterised by:

- a deliberate manipulation of a range of sentence structures – conscious control of sentence variety for effect
- a proficiently handled range of punctuation that enhances the writing
- accurate spelling of most words
- an extended vocabulary which is employed with increasing precision.

Competence level 4 [7–8]
Characterised by:

- an assured use of a wide range of sentence structures that enhances the overall effect of the writing in terms of clarity, purpose and audience
- confident deployment of a full range of punctuation that facilitates fluency and complements meaning
- an extended, apposite vocabulary used with precision – errors will be one-off mistakes or, occasionally, the outcome of ambitious attempts to use complex language.

Higher Unit 1 Section B

Task 2: Reading Multi-modal Texts (maximum of 9 marks)

Response time: 10 minutes

Compare and contrast how **presentational devices** are used in **both** to make these centres appeal to the reader. Analyse the use of **images, colour** and the layout.

What follows is a task-specific checklist of evidence relating to the Assessment Objectives for Studying Written Language/Reading. This contains examples of the types of material that candidates at all competence levels may be expected to include in their responses.

The use made of images and colour:

- Quorn Hall's main image of archery is quite restrained whereas Todd's Leap presents multiple images of teenagers and young adults experiencing a range of dramatic activities. The images have been selected to attract quite different target audiences: Quorn is a residential facility aimed at visiting parties of students whilst Todd's Leap is targeting teenagers/young adults seeking an adrenaline-filled day's fun.
- The Todd's Leap inside spread is more visually striking with its multiple white bordered images set against the contrasting mud coloured backdrop and various font styles and colours which contrast to the more formal layout of the Quorn material, although its minor images are emphasised by their 'star' surrounds.
- Quorn Hall's main image (the teenage archer directs the reader's eye to the remainder of the centre spread) is supported by four minor images (all are quite placid/static in nature); unlike the series of images used by Todd's Leap (some blurred to create the sense of dramatic action/others of young people in mid-activity) and white silhouettes (all of young people in action-packed poses) as well as background colour and design (tyre tracks to generate a sense of the variety of exciting activities on offer).

The layout:

- The Quorn Hall inside spread relies on a more information-based approach rather the approach of Todd's Leap which uses the inside spread primarily as an image based piece of promotional advertising.
- Quorn Hall has opted for a 'cleaner', more conservative, restrained look – a white background with one major image supported by some smaller images. By contrast, Todd's Leap has made much greater use of images to highlight its range of activities that are presented informally as angled overlapping images surrounding a central block information (conventional black on white in the case of Quorn and striking, less formal white on brown in Todd's Leap). Their different purposes are again evident in these choices.
- The heading are very different. Quorn Hall's is minimal and formal in its feel whilst Todd's Leap employs a range of fonts at different angles, font sizes, styles and colours, all to support the sense of excitement and variety.
- The font styles are very different. Quorn Hall is formal, clear and uncluttered, in contrast to Todd's Leap which generates a more informal feel, creating the impression that this centre is crammed full of exciting activities.
- The layout of the text is quite similar. Images attract the eye and engage the reader and the remainder of the spread is given over to short paragraphs of text, both formally laid out using sub-headings for guidance.
- Both Quorn Hall and Todd's Leap rely on subheadings to enable their readers to navigate the information effectively. In Quorn Hall's case these are tied in thematically with the green used in the remainder of the centre spread. By contrast, in Todd's Leap, orange sub-headings appear to be employed simply because they standout against the dark background.

Competence level 1 [1–3]
Characterised by:

- a sound overall evaluation of how some of the presentational devices achieve their effects
- a straightforward explanation and comparison of how these devices have been used to engage and influence the reader positively
- the development of an appropriate interpretation of the stimulus material through an uncomplicated drawing together of mainly appropriate evidence.

Competence level 2 [4–6]
Characterised by:

- a clear evaluation of how the presentational devices have been deployed to achieve their effects
- a competent explanation of how these devices have been manipulated to engage and influence the reader positively
- the development of an accurate interpretation of the stimulus materials through a drawing together of a range of appropriate evidence from both sources.

Competence level 3 [7–9]
Characterised by:

- an assured evaluation of how the presentational devices have been deployed to achieve their particular effects
- a confident explanation and comparison of how these devices interact to positively influence the target audience
- the development of an perceptive interpretation of the stimulus material through a purposeful comparison of a range of precisely selected, supporting evidence.

Task 3: Reading Multi-Modal Texts (maximum of 15 marks)

Response time: 20 minutes

Compare and contrast how **language** has been used in **both** brochures to inform the reader and promote what each centre has to offer.

What follows is a task-specific checklist of evidence relating to the Assessment Objectives for Studying Written Language/Reading (see page 57). This contains examples of the types of material that candidates at all competence levels may be expected to include in their responses.

How language is employed:

- The Quorn inside spread uses formal language in quite complex sentences: 'Supported activities can be arranged in conjunction with...'/'Adjacent to the Hall is the River Soar...'; in contrast, Todd's Leap use a much more informal and direct style, beginning in their headings: 'Now are you ready for some serious fun?'/'Game on!!!'/'...an experience you'll, never forget!!!' Direct address, questions and use of exclamation marks for exaggeration, emphasis and immediacy abound — credit references to relevant, focused examples.

- The Quorn text is quite detached in its approach: 'There is ample space to relax and enjoy the scenery'/'a cold meal can be provided by prior arrangement': by marked contrast Todd's Leap is consistently positive, assertive and inviting in tone: 'The classic Rodeo Bull is always a winner...'/'Finish off the day on a real high...'

- Quorn Hall's brochure uses a formal, impersonal tone: 'Quorn Hall (not 'We') caters primarily for student groups' whereas Todd's Leap employs a direct, conversational tone which is designed to be friendly and encouraging: 'If you fancy yourself as Robin Hood...'/'Prepare for highflying fun as you harness...'

- Todd's Leap uses an initial question to engage their readers 'Now, are you ready for some serious fun?' whereas Quorn Hall open with a formal statement: 'Quorn Hall International Centre can offer...'

- Todd's Leap uses language to build a rapport, generate excitement and anticipation: 'digging holes... a 'hole' lot of fun!' (a pun)/'thrilling, action packed Zip Line adventure'/'Become fascinated by...' (use of imperative); whereas the language in the Quorn leaflet is neutral: 'The Hall was built as a family... eventually purchased...'/its most positive claim is that: 'Quorn Hall catering is a speciality'.

- Safety is an issue about which both seek to reassure the reader: Quorn Hall state they have 'fully qualified/teachers/instructors'; Todd's Leap finish with 'you are in good [safe] hands!'

Competence level 1 [1–5]
Characterised by:

- a sound overall evaluation of how some of the language and the manner in which it is constructed achieve effects

- a straightforward explanation of how these devices have been used to engage the audience

- the development of an appropriate interpretation of the stimulus material through an uncomplicated drawing together of mainly appropriate supporting evidence from both sources.

Competence level 2 [6–10]
Characterised by:

- a clear evaluation of how language and the way in which it is structured has been deployed to achieve effects

- a competent explanation of how these devices have been used in an attempt to engage and manipulate the audience

- the development of an accurate interpretation of the stimulus through a drawing together of a range of appropriate supporting evidence from both sources.

Competence level 3 [11–15]
Characterised by:

- an assured evaluation of how language use, as well as grammatical and structural devices, have been deployed to achieve their particular effects

- a confident explanation of how these devices interact to positively influence the target audience

- the development of a perceptive interpretation of the stimulus material through a purposeful comparison of a range of precisely selected supporting evidence.

Unit 2

Sample questions and mark schemes

Unit 2 Foundation Tier (90 minutes)

 Section A: Functional Writing

Up to **16 marks** are available for an organised, appropriate and interesting response.

Up to **8 marks** are available for the use of a range of sentence structures and correct spelling, punctuation and grammar.

Task 1

Write the talk you would give to a group of young adults who are about to begin teacher training.

Based on your own experiences, write the talk you would give to them on:

● the teaching that you found was effective
● the teaching methods they would be advised to avoid in their teaching. **[24]**

Planning your answer. . .

It is suggested that you organise your time like this:

● **5–10 minutes** planning and organising your ideas
● **25–30 minutes** writing your talk
● **5 minutes** checking over your response.

Section B: Reading Non-Fiction

Read the following text from an advertisement promoting the reading of magazines. This is written in a manner that is designed to sustain the reader's interest. (The text is printed on page 87.)

Task 2

Explain how the writer holds the reader's interest.

In your answer show how the writer has:

● used a style of writing that is lively and personal

● included an interesting mix of facts and opinions

● selected words and phrases for effect

● made use of sentence structuring and paragraphing. **[24]**

This is not the Internet.
Feel free to curl up and settle in.

Magazines don't blink on and off. They don't show video or deliver ads that pop up out of nowhere. You can't DVR magazines and you can't play games on them.

But you can take one to the beach, to bed or just about anywhere else and, chances are, it will engage, entertain and enlighten you in ways no other medium can.

Perhaps that explains why magazine readership has actually increased versus five years ago. The top 25 magazines continue to reach a wider audience than the top 25 prime-time TV shows. And despite the escalating war for consumers' eyeballs, readers spend an average of 43 minutes per issue.

What accounts for this ongoing attraction? Why do nine out of ten American adults choose to spend so much time with an unabashedly analog medium? ☆

One enduring truth: people of every age love the experience of reading a magazine, even when the same content is available online. So curl up, get comfortable and enjoy the rest of this magazine.

The *Power* of *Print*®

☆ *unabashedly analog medium*: a means of communicating that is unashamedly based on simply reading images and text

Unit 2 Higher Tier (90 minutes)

Section A: Functional Writing

Up to **16 marks** are available for an organised, appropriate and interesting response.

Up to **8 marks** are available for the use of a range of sentence structures and correct spelling, punctuation and grammar.

Task 1

Compose a letter to a national newspaper. In this letter argue for OR against P.E. and Sport being given a place in schools' timetables.

[24]

Planning your answer. . .

Below are some ideas you might want to think about as you plan your response.

Education is there to develop the whole individual – that includes our physical well-being too!

Do you have any idea of the dread and humiliation anxious teenagers suffer in changing rooms??

Have you ever heard of the phrase 'a team player'? This ability is one of sport's most valuable lessons.

I'm no good at sport and I never will be – so why am I expected to make a fool of myself on a weekly basis?

P.E. and Sport in School

There's a sport for everyone – just because you haven't found it yet is no reason to stop searching!!

I can get all the activity I need on an Xbox – I'll stay out of the rain and mud thanks!

There's more bullying results from sport than any of that nonsense about team players – co-operating with others is a matter of civilised behaviour and has nothing to do with sport!

Sport can build individual self-esteem and confidence as well as teaching us valuable lessons about preparing in order to succeed!

Section B: Reading Non-Fiction

Read the following excerpt from a travel writer who is describing a walk he was taking on Inishmore, the largest of the Aran Islands off Galway.   **[24]**

Task 2

Explain how the writer holds the reader's interest. In your answer show how the writer has:

- used a style of writing that is lively and personal

- included an interesting mix of personal observations

- selected words and phrases for effect and made use of sentence structuring and paragraphing.

Everyone who passes – pedestrians, farmers in tractors, pony and trap drivers – says hello, as they have on every lane and track and path I've travelled so far this trip. Like the mundane shopping transaction that becomes a social occasion, this makes a refreshing change from the south of England [This is where the writer actually lives].

I go walking a lot on the South Downs Way, a wonderful Neolithic pathway across the chalklands that look down on the English Channel. Once you get away from the car parks where dog owners take their half-mad pets, deranged from incarceration in suburbia [being unable to get out and run about in their middle-class housing estates] to relieve themselves, and attack sheep and horse-back riders, the path is surprisingly empty, even in the height of summer. On top of the Downs you can see for hundreds of yards ahead so you always know when someone else is approaching. For several minutes you watch each other getting closer; and then, as you're about to pass, the other person suddenly develops a deep interest in something in the hedge or on their boot, and tries to pretend they haven't seen you.

'*Hello!*' I bellow with the most aggressive smile I can muster.

'Oh,' they fluster, feigning surprise. 'Er, yes. Hello.' Occasionally, the posher, older hikers will simply grunt and stare, as if you've come up the drive to the front door when you should have used the tradesmen's entrance. What do you mean, hello? they're thinking. I refuse to acknowledge the existence of someone who may not be my social equal.

Perhaps I'm being hard on the English. They, or we, are a very private race, which isn't something of which you could ever accuse the Irish. I think it'd be impossible for one stranger to pass another in rural Ireland and not acknowledge the moment, and this is one of the defining differences between our two nations.

The dogs are different, too. I've passed several on this afternoon's walk, and not one of them has even bothered to bark. One actually walked with me for half a mile to keep me company. They don't seem to have caught on to the notion that prevails among dogs in the rest of Europe – that they're meant to be defending stuff from you. They will, however, chase any car that passes, though I suspect this may be a legal requirement enforceable by the gardai.

'Ah, good evening Mrs O'Riordan. Sorry to be bothering you, but I hear a Toyota Corolla went past earlier today, and Buru just lay there like a plank.'

'I'm sorry about that now, Sergeant. Next time I'll smack him with a hurley.'

'Good luck, now.'

'Good luck.'

From *McCarthy's Bar*, Pete McCarthy

Foundation Unit 2 Section A

Task 1: Functional Writing 1st assessment (maximum of 16 marks)

Response time: 45 minutes

Write the talk you would give to a group of young adults who are about to begin teacher training.

This task-specific checklist outlines the writing skills associated with Writing AO i and ii that candidates at all competence levels may be expected to attempt to employ in their responses. Credit any other valid strategies used that are not mentioned below.

Communicate clearly and effectively and imaginatively, demonstrating:

- a handling of the topic in such a way as to attempt to positively develop the reader's interest
- use of a style that endeavours to build a positive relationship with the target audience
- possible use of anecdotes/humour to engage the audience.

Adapting form and vocabulary to task and purpose in ways that engage the reader, demonstrating:

- an awareness of the audience
- a use of tone that is meant to engage and sustain the audience's attention
- use of a straightforward vocabulary that is in keeping with the task and audience and that, occasionally, may enliven the writing.

Organise information and ideas into structured, sequenced sentences, paragraphs and whole texts, demonstrating:

- a sense of progression – the reader being taken through the writer's point of view
- an awareness of opening and closing paragraphs
- some use of topic sentences for different paragraphs
- development that uses organisation in an attempt to hold the audience's interest.

Use a variety of linguistic and structural features for cohesion and coherence, demonstrating:

- some variety of sentence length for effect
- occasional use of connectives to give coherence to paragraphing
- the use of rhetorical devices – the rule of three, questions, hyperbole, etc.

Competence level 1 [1–4]
Characterised by:

- some general, rather sketchy development of his/her views on the issue
- an unconvincing grasp of purpose and audience
- some attempt at simple structuring using a rudimentary style.

Competence level 2 [5–8]
Characterised by:

- a simple development, relating his/her views about the issue in an elementary manner
- a broad sense of purpose and/or audience that may not be sustained
- a basic structuring and an elementary style.

Competence level 3 [9–12]
Characterised by:

- an uncomplicated development, relating his/her point of view in a deliberate fashion
- an unsophisticated understanding of purpose and audience
- a logical structuring and a straightforward style.

Competence level 4 [13–16]
Characterised by:

- a generally effective development that maintains the reader's interest in the subject
- a recognition of purpose and audience
- a clear structuring and an increasingly fluent style.

Task 1: Functional Writing 2nd assessment (maximum of 8 marks)

This task-specific checklist outlines the writing skills associated with Writing AO iii that candidates at all competence levels may be expected to attempt to employ in their responses.

Credit any other valid strategies used that are not mentioned below.

The range and effectiveness of the sentence structures used:

- The wider the control that a candidate exhibits with regard to sentence structuring, the greater is his/her ability to sustain interest and establish a rapport with the examiner.
- The more competent and varied that manipulation of sentence structure is, the higher will be the mark awarded.

The use made of accurate punctuation and spelling:

- Part of the fabric of sentence structure is the control that comes from the accurate use of appropriate punctuation. Here too there is scope for variety that can help to engage the examiner. The greater the range of punctuation appropriately used, the higher will be the reward.
- Accuracy in spelling is, in isolation, potentially misleading; it needs to be viewed in conjunction with the range and precision of the vocabulary that a candidate draws upon. A limited and mundane vocabulary spelt with unerring accuracy is unlikely to capture the examiner's attention. Credit attempts to use vocabulary ambitiously where the word may not always be accurately spelt but has been chosen with care.

Competence level 1 [1–2]

Characterised by:

- little control of sentence structuring – instead, simple connectives used to link ideas; verbs often repeated
- occasional use of full stops and commas tends to be the limit of punctuation
- some accuracy in the spelling of simple words
- the range of vocabulary is narrow.

Competence level 2 [3–4]

Characterised by:

- a use of basic sentence structuring that offers little variation in construction or length
- generally correct use of full stops and the use of some other forms of punctuation
- basic vocabulary is usually spelt accurately
- a limited vocabulary.

Competence level 3 [5–6]

Characterised by:

- a controlled use of straightforward sentence structuring – there will be evidence of some variety in sentence construction and length
- a generally secure use of basic punctuation to support structure
- generally accurate spelling of straightforward, regular vocabulary
- an uncomplicated vocabulary will be evident.

Competence level 4 [7–8]

Characterised by:

- increasingly sustained competence in the handling of a variety of sentence structures – occasionally these may be used for effect
- the basics of punctuation – full stops, commas, exclamation and question marks – used accurately, adding clarity to the work
- generally accurate spelling including some words with irregular patterns
- a greater precision in the use of a widening vocabulary.

Foundation Unit 2 Section B

Task 2: Reading Non-Fiction (maximum of 24 marks)

Response time: 20 minutes

Read the following text from an advertisement promoting the reading of magazines. This is written in a manner that is designed to hold the reader's interest.

This task-specific checklist outlines the material candidates across the competence levels may be expected to include in their responses. Credit fully any other valid suggestions/comments.

The lively and personal style:

- The two sentences in the headline initially attract our attention – they cleverly reflect the opening and closing points in the text.
- The direct voice adopted by the narrator draws the reader in: 'You can't DVR magazines.'
- The opening paragraph consists of four brief, blunt, negative statements about what can't be done with a magazine. These then immediately contrast with the second paragraph which consists solely of a list of the positive qualities magazines possess.
- The easy conversational nature of the writing: for example, starting the second paragraph with the conjunction 'But'.
- The piece is written demonstrating a clear sense of progression/development – the paragraph connectives illustrate this.

The use made of fact and opinion:

- The writer makes a quite striking initial contrast through the use of straightforward facts in the two opening paragraphs: 'They don't show video' in contrast with: 'you can take one to the beach'.
- The writer relies upon the use of facts to create effect. The third paragraph is built around what the writer clearly thinks are a series of startling facts that will impress the reader as well as also affirming the popularity of reading: 'magazine readership has actually increased'/ 'the top 25 magazines continue to. . .'/ 'readers spent an average of. . .'
- Not all the statements used are factual, for example there is an extravagant opinion at the end of the second paragraph: 'chances are, it will engage, entertain and enlighten you in ways no other medium can'.
- The last paragraph is presented as the logical conclusion to the preceding series of facts. The writer, however, is presenting a sweeping opinion as if it were fact: 'One enduring truth: people of every age love the experience of reading a magazine. . .'

The selection of words and phrases for effect:

- The writer uses vocabulary to lead the reader through his/her argument: 'Perhaps that explains why. . .'
- Repetition plays a significant role in the opening paragraph: 'don't' and 'can't'.
- The language is accessible; however, the use of 'unabashedly analog medium' is in stark contrast to the remainder of the text.
- The following metaphor is as colourful as the language becomes: 'the escalating war for consumers' eyeballs'.
- The opening to the final paragraph, 'One enduring truth' is rather over-the-top given the subject matter.

The use made of sentence structuring and paragraphing

- The length of the sentences and the paragraphs matches the purpose and audience. This is an advertisement and so the sentences tend to be short and the paragraphs are equally brief to maintain an 'easy' level of readability.
- The contrast already mentioned between the content in the first two paragraphs is also further reinforced by their contrasting sentence structures. Both paragraphs are about the same length; however, the first paragraph consists of three short sentences whereas the second paragraph is a much longer single sentence in the form of a list.
- The fourth paragraph consists of back-to-back questions to direct the reader's focus and develop the writer's point of view.

Competence level 1 [1–6]
Characterised by:
- basic comments in relation to some of the features in the bullet points
- reporting offers some simple points that may be supported from the text
- simple interpretation of some features.

Competence level 2 [7–12]
Characterised by:
- a very straightforward consideration of most features in the bullet points
- some basic analysis that may be supported by appropriate evidence
- some development of valid, if simple, interpretations occasionally supported by straightforward evidence.

Competence level 3 [13–18]
Characterised by:
- a consideration of the features highlighted in the bullet points in relation to the desired outcome – sustaining the reader's interest
- straightforward analysis supported by uncomplicated explanations
- appropriately developed interpretations backed up by mainly straightforward supporting evidence.

Competence level 4 [19–24]
Characterised by:
- some analysis of the bullet points
- an examination that will be supported by appropriate explanations
- the development of a competent interpretation of the stimulus material through appropriate supporting evidence.

Higher Unit 2 Section A

Task 1: Functional Writing 1st assessment (maximum of 16 marks)

Response time: 45 minutes

Compose a letter to a national newspaper. In this letter argue for OR against P.E. and sport being given a place in schools' timetables.

This task-specific checklist outlines the writing skills associated with Writing AO i and ii that candidates at all competence levels may be expected to attempt to employ in their responses.

Communicate clearly and effectively and imaginatively, demonstrating:

- a handling of the topic in such a way as to positively develop the reader's interest
- use of a style that builds a positive relationship with the target audience
- use of anecdotal evidence to enliven the writing and engage the audience.

Adapting form and vocabulary to task and purpose in ways that engage the reader, demonstrating:

- a conscious awareness of the newspaper reader as audience
- a use of tone that is designed to engage and sustain the audience's attention
- use of vocabulary that is in keeping with the task and audience to enhance, enrich and enliven the writing.

Organise information and ideas into structured, sequenced sentences, paragraphs and whole texts demonstrating:

- a sense of logical progression – the reader being led through the writer's point of view/thoughts
- the use of opening and closing paragraphs
- the deployment of topic sentences for different paragraphs
- development that uses conscious organisation to sustain the audience's interest.

Use a variety linguistic and structural features for cohesion and coherence demonstrating:

- a conscious varying of sentence length for effect
- the use of connectives to give coherence to paragraphing
- the use of rhetorical devices such as the rule of three, questions, etc., to develop interest and a rapport with the audience.

Competence level 1 [1–4]
Characterised by:

- an uncomplicated development, that presents his/her point of view
- a general sense of purpose and audience
- a logical structuring and a straightforward style.

Competence level 2 [5–8]
Characterised by:

- a generally effective development that maintains the reader's interest
- a recognition of purpose and audience
- a clear structuring and an increasingly fluent style.

Competence level 3 [9–12]
Characterised by:

- a competent development that clearly engages with the reader
- a confident awareness of purpose and audience
- proficiently structured writing with evidence of a developing, lively style.

Competence level 4 [13–16]
Characterised by:

- a poised and sophisticated development that commands the reader's attention throughout
- a positive rapport with the audience
- assured competence in terms of structure underpinned by a confident style.

Task 1: Functional Writing 2nd assessment (maximum of 8 marks)

This task-specific checklist outlines the writing skills associated with Writing AO iii that candidates at all competence levels may be expected to attempt to employ in their responses.

The range and effectiveness of sentence structures:

- The wider the repertoire and greater the degree of originality and control that a candidate exhibits with regard to sentence structuring, the greater is his/her ability to sustain interest and establish a rapport with the examiner. The fresher, the more assured and varied that manipulation of sentence structure is, the higher will be the mark awarded.

The use made of accurate punctuation and spelling:

- Part of the fabric of sentence structure is the control that comes from the accurate use of appropriate punctuation. Here too there is scope for variety and creativity that can help to engage the examiner. The greater the range and innovation in relation to the use of punctuation, the higher will be the reward.

- Accuracy in spelling is, in isolation, potentially misleading; it needs to be viewed in conjunction with the range and precision of the vocabulary that a candidate draws upon. A limited and mundane vocabulary spelt with unerring accuracy is unlikely to capture the examiner's attention. Credit ambitious use of vocabulary where the word may not always be accurately spelt but has been chosen with care to capture the essence of a situation.

Competence level 1 [1–2]

Characterised by:

- a controlled use of straightforward sentence structuring – there will be evidence of some variety in sentence construction and length
- a generally secure use of basic punctuation to support structure
- generally accurate spelling of straightforward, regular vocabulary
- an uncomplicated vocabulary will be evident.

Competence level 2 [3–4]

Characterised by:

- increasingly sustained competence in the handling of a variety of sentence structures – occasionally these may be used for effect
- the basics of punctuation – full stops, commas, exclamation and question marks – used accurately, adding clarity to the work
- generally accurate spelling including some words with irregular patterns
- a greater precision in the use of a widening vocabulary.

Competence level 3 [5–6]

Characterised by:

- a deliberate manipulation of a range sentence structures – conscious control of sentence variety for effect
- a proficiently handled range of punctuation that enhances the writing
- accurate spelling of most words
- an extended vocabulary which is employed with increasing precision.

Competence level 4 [7–8]

Characterised by:

- an assured use of a wide range of sentence structures that enhances the overall effect of the writing in terms of clarity, purpose and audience
- confident deployment of a full range of punctuation that aids fluency and complements meaning
- an extended, apposite vocabulary used with precision – errors will be one-off mistakes or, occasionally, the outcome of ambitious attempts to use complex language.

Higher Unit 2 Section B

Task 2: Reading Non-Fiction (maximum of 24 marks)

Response time: 45 minutes

Explain how the writer holds the reader's interest. In your answer show how the writer has: used a style of writing that is lively and personal/included an interesting mix of personal observations/selected words and phrases for effect/and made use of sentence structuring and paragraphing.

This task-specific checklist of evidence that outlines the material candidates across the competence levels may be expected to include in their responses. Credit fully any other valid suggestions/ comments.

The lively and personal style:
- The direct voice adopted from the beginning by the narrator draws the reader in 'Everyone that passes...'
- The two lists in the opening sentence emphasise the writer's point and the opening to the second paragraph continues this personal approach with its first-person narration of a personal anecdote: 'I go walking a lot on the South Downs'.
- The anecdotes are used to illustrate the writer's opinions: 'one of the defining differences between our two nations'.
- The conversational tone is allied to a sense that we are taken into the writer's confidence: 'Perhaps I'm being . . . English.'
- The eccentric, exaggerated descriptions sustain the reader's attention: 'relieve themselves, and attack sheep and horse-back riders'.
- The use of conversations allow the writer to highlight the ridiculous nature of situations: ' "Hello!" I bellow.'

The interesting mix of personal observations and humour:
- The whole piece is built around a series of anecdotes and engaging observations that allow the writer to highlight the differences between the Irish and the English: 'the mundane shopping transaction that becomes a social occasion'.
- The use of exaggeration to create comic effect: 'attack sheep and horse-back riders'/ '"I'll smack him with a hurley."'
- The writer apportions motives to strangers which are entertaining: 'you should have used the tradesmen's entrance'.
- The use of direct speech adds humour to anecdotes: 'Ah, good evening Mrs O'Riordan.'
- The writer's engaging eccentricity: 'I suspect this may be a legal requirement enforceable by the gardai.'
- The imaginary chat between the gardai sergeant and Mrs O'Riordan with its outrageous conclusion is humorous.

The selection of words and phrases for effect and the use made of sentence structuring and paragraphing:
- The writer uses vocabulary to lead the reader through his experiences: 'they fluster, feigning surprise'/ 'as you're about to pass, the other person suddenly develops a deep interest in something in the hedge'.
- The personal nature is reflected in his use of what others are thinking: 'What do you mean, hello? they're thinking'.
- The language is generally informal, accessible and conversational: ' "they're meant to be defending stuff from you."
- There is also evidence that a quite extensive range of vocabulary is used: 'the mundane shopping transaction that becomes a social occasion'/ 'deranged from incarceration in suburbia'.
- The writer's enthusiasm and concise use of language is evident: 'a wonderful Neolithic pathway . . . the English Channel'.
- The range and length of sentences in this travel writing match purpose and audience; they vary from the relatively short, conversational offerings: 'The dogs are different, too.' to the complex: 'Once you get away . . . the height of summer.'
- The paragraphs track the development of the writer's thoughts. This is clearly exemplified in the fourth and fifth paragraphs as the piece moves on, amusingly, to note that the differences are not only reflected in the people but in their dogs!

Competence level 1 [1–6]
Characterised by:
- a consideration of the features highlighted in the bullet points in relation to the desired outcome – sustaining the reader's interest
- straightforward analysis that will be supported by uncomplicated explanations
- appropriately developed interpretations backed up by mainly straightforward supporting evidence.

Competence level 2 [7–12]
Characterised by:
- an analysis of the features highlighted in the bullet points
- an examination that will be supported by appropriate explanations
- the development of a competent interpretation of the stimulus material through the presentation of appropriate supporting evidence.

Competence level 3 [13–18]
Characterised by:
- an evaluation of the features highlighted in the bullet points
- an assessment that will employ confident explanations
- the development of an accurate interpretation of the stimulus material through the presentation of a range of valid supporting evidence.

Competence level 4 [19–24]
Characterised by:
- an assured evaluation of features in the bullet points
- a secure explanation that will utilise perceptive explanations
- the development of an assured interpretation through the drawing together of a range of precisely selected, accurate, supporting evidence.